Self Development for Sales People

Patrick Forsyth

SALES

12.10

T0341417

- Fast-track route to effective and customized selling approaches. Provides an antidote to selling today's products with yesterday's techniques

- Covers how to create and implement a plan of self development, from attitudes and approaches to skills improvement, designed to keep sales people at the leading edge of professionalism and success

- Full of best practice examples and case studies to get the individual started

- Includes a comprehensive resources guide, key concepts and thinkers, a 10-step action plan for self-development, and a section of FAQs

≫EXPRESS EXEC.COM≪
essential management thinking at your fingertips

The right of Patrick Forsyth to be identified as the author of this book has been asserted in accordance with the Copyright, Designs and Patents Act 1988

First Published 2003 by
Capstone Publishing Limited (a Wiley company)
8 Newtec Place
Magdalen Road
Oxford OX4 1RE
United Kingdom
http://www.capstoneideas.com

CIP catalogue records for this book are available from the British Library and the US Library of Congress

ISBN 1-84112-453-2

Wiley also publishes its books in a variety of electronic formats. Some content that appears in print may not be available in electronic books.

Websites often change their contents and addresses; details of sites listed in this book were accurate at the time of writing, but may change.

Substantial discounts on bulk quantities of Capstone Books are available to corporations, professional associations and other organizations. For details telephone Capstone Publishing on (+44-1865-798623), fax (+44-1865-240941) or email (info@wiley-capstone.co.uk).

Contents

Introduction to ExpressExec

ExpressExec is a completely up-to-date resource of current business practice, accessible in a number of ways – anytime, anyplace, anywhere. ExpressExec combines best practice cases, key ideas, action points, glossaries, further reading, and resources.

Each module contains 10 individual titles that cover all the key aspects of global business practice. Written by leading experts in their field, the knowledge imparted provides executives with the tools and skills to increase their personal and business effectiveness, benefiting both employee and employer.

ExpressExec is available in a number of formats:

» **Print** – 120 titles available through retailers or printed on demand using any combination of the 1200 chapters available.
» **E-Books** – e-books can be individually downloaded from ExpressExec.com or online retailers onto PCs, handheld computers, and e-readers.
» **Online** – http://www.expressexec.wiley.com/ provides fully searchable access to the complete ExpressExec resource via the Internet – a cost-effective online tool to increase business expertise across a whole organization.

» **ExpressExec Performance Support Solution (EEPSS)** - a software solution that integrates ExpressExec content with interactive tools to provide organizations with a complete internal management development solution.

» **ExpressExec Rights and Syndication** - ExpressExec content can be licensed for translation or display within intranets or on Internet sites.

To find out more visit www.ExpressExec.com or contact elound@wiley-capstone.co.uk.

Introduction to Self Development for Sales People

This chapter makes it clear that it is the individual rather than the organization or employer that is addressed in the book. It also considers the separate factors in the sales process.

"Success doesn't come to you, you go to it."

Marva Calins

Whatever job you may do the maxim quoted above is not a bad one to adopt. The world does not owe you a living. Nor these days can you realistically assume that every assistance will be forthcoming from an organization (if one such employs you) intent on doing everything possible to further your career, or even to assist you perform the job you do for them currently satisfactorily. You need to take the initiative and adopt an active approach to developing your competence to do what you need to be able to do now, and what you want to be able to do in the future.

To a degree this is true of every job. Here, in the context of the sales jobs on which we focus there are even more pressing reasons to adopt this view, reasons that stem from the very nature of the sales process. Before examining that, however, let us make it clear to whom this book is addressed.

First, it is addressed to the individual rather than the organization or employer. It makes reference to the organization, of course, but the focus is on the individual and on individual action: on you and what you can do. Secondly it interprets the sales role broadly. It is thus designed to be useful to:

» those doing full time sales jobs in whatever form and at whatever level. This includes field sales staff, account managers and those working in particular ways, such as telephone sales people. It also includes sales managers, those managing a team of such people; and
» anyone for whom sales skill is important, and who has sales responsibilities within their job portfolio. This includes managers, even senior managers and managing directors, who for reasons of the size or nature of their businesses take on sales tasks.

Thus, if your success is to any degree dependent – or will be in the future – on successfully persuading others to do business with you and your organization, then this book is aimed at you. If you see your sales role as a step along the way in a career you aim to take further, then the first job is surely to excel at what you do now (though you could also look at the *ExpressExec* title *Career Management*).

That said it does not set out to instruct you on how to sell (other titles in this series do that), it looks at how to make what you do and how you do it successful; and at how to make it go on being successful over time. Why is this so important? It is not just because of the competitive nature of the modern work environment, other reasons stem from the very nature of the sales process.

THE SALES PROCESS

Selling successfully was never easy. In today's competitive markets it can be damned difficult. Beyond that, however, three separate factors make self development in the sales area especially important.

Selling is:

» *complex:* selling is multifaceted. To sell successfully you must communicate well, and do so persuasively. You must understand customers, what they expect, how they think and how they act. You must know your industry, products or services, company and customers' situation inside out. You must manage individual sales meetings well, and often you must do the same for the whole strategic process of developing major customers or negotiating major complex sales over what may be long lead times. And more no doubt. Despite the tendency of some people to underestimate the complexity of selling (or to see it as a poor relation to more sophisticated marketing techniques, perhaps with an unsavory image – pushy sales people), it is a vital part of marketing that demands a great deal of those people who do it. In this light it is hardly surprising that it needs working at in order to make it successful;

» *dynamic:* the nature of everything about selling – markets, custo-mers, competition and more – is dynamic. We live in a fast-changing world. Sales approaches and techniques may work well today with one customer, but such is no guarantee that an identical way will work equally well tomorrow with a different customer. Things change. First, sales approaches need to be individually deployed; that is, the best possible approach must be selected and used for a particular situation. Secondly, the situations in which selling must operate, and be made effective, will change over time. All this means that the process of keeping up to date is continuous and essentially endless; you can spend a lifetime learning to sell in different ways in an endeavor to maximize effectiveness; and

» *fragile:* selling demands precision. A sale may be won or lost on minor differences of approach. Just using one word or phrase rather than another may be enough to change the response. Care is always necessary and again this means that the sales person benefits from being able to exercise this care as an almost automatic part of their approach. The best sales people are inherently conscious of how they do things and of how things need to be done. This too means that an active approach to fine tuning skills can pay dividends.

Everything said about these three factors combines to explain why this is an area where a conscious and active approach to self development is essential.

If you sell, then however you may describe the task (and the image of selling creates a range of euphemisms, many a sales person is a "customer services executive"), you must do it well. The very nature of the process means that success is always to be laid primarily at your door; so too is failure.

You have to get it right, and you may get no second chances.

Whatever your expertise at present, its nature and level will need to change. This may mean major extension if you are a newcomer to the field, or it may mean what is better described as fine-tuning – though this may still be of considerable significance and influence ultimate success very much.

So, you must ensure this change takes place. You must ensure that your knowledge is kept up to date, your expertise and skill continue to be finely tuned and that you are able to do an equally outstanding job tomorrow, next week or next year whatever new circumstances you face.

The remainder of this book reviews how you can achieve just that. It looks at what makes the process manageable, and what makes it effective. For the sales person wanting to be – or remain – successful, inaction in terms of self-development is simply not an option. Perhaps we might wish otherwise, but as Beverly Sills said: "There are no shortcuts to any place worth going."

What is
Self Development
in Sales?

This chapter considers the following concepts relating to self development in sales:

» the development process;
» the methods; and
» the results.

''It's what you learn after you know it all that counts.''

John Wooden

Self development implies a process directed at improvement. In a job context this in turn implies the aim of improving specific job performance and thus incorporating or extending the skills that make that possible. The introductory section reviewed the many reasons why such a process is necessary, here we examine something of the detail of how it can be made to happen. It needs more than some kind of good intention. To be effective the process needs to be:

» consciously entered into;
» well planned;
» systematically executed; and
» focused on clear objectives and intended to make a real and tangible difference.

Having said that, it should be acknowledged immediately that alongside the specific objectives there are – or should be – more personal and intangible ones. Self development can make your job more interesting, satisfying and fun. And it can also help your longer-term career progress and help your overall advancement.

In a busy life an activity like self development must not be a chore, especially not an impossible one, so approaches to it must make it manageable. As Chapter 1 made clear, spending time on self development is not a nice option or something to do a little if time permits; it is a necessity. Your success and future prosperity depends on it; the only question is how much activity is necessary and what should this be?

The answer to this comes, in part, from an understanding and utilization of the development process.

THE DEVELOPMENT PROCESS

In sales the evidence of results, whether good or bad, is clear. Though some development activity may stem from a more general look ahead, much of it will come from an examination of the current situation. Managers are charged with monitoring the performance of their staff, and the systematic way that they go about this can equally be applied to oneself. Consider the formal process first; the following stages can be identified.

» *Examine job description:* this allows you to review the levels of knowledge and skills that a particular job demands, and the attitudes required of the person who does it. This states the ideal and the current position and is not, at this stage, linked to the individual currently doing the job.

» *Examine the person:* this enables a look, alongside the ideal, at what the situation actually is currently. How do the knowledge, skills and attitudes of the individual stack up alongside what the job demands? This information comes from observation of the person, their performance and their results. Formal appraisal is a key part of this, as is other, less formal, evaluation.

» *Look to the future:* before reaching any conclusions from the process described so far, it is necessary also to think ahead, again focusing on the job rather than the individual. What will the job demand in future that will be different from the current situation? What developments (in the organization, in technology in the market and expectation of customers – and more) are coming? Specifically what new skills, knowledge or attitudes will be necessary, and how will existing ones need to change?

» *Defining the gap:* together two factors coming from the above may define a gap: the combination of any shortfall in current levels of competence plus the need to add to this in future. This is the so-called development (or training) gap and gives you the area towards which development must be directed with any individual.

Of course, the picture produced may be fine; no immediate action may be necessary. In so dynamic an area of work as sales, the reality is most likely that some action – major or minor – is necessary. If so a plan of action is needed to deal with implementation. Again viewing this systematically provides a simple checklist approach as to what to do.

» *List what needs to be addressed:* whatever is identified, from minor matters that need only a small input to the development of new skills that must be approached from square one.

» *Rate the list in terms of priorities:* in most organizations resources (time, money and training facilities) are finite. It is unlikely to be possible to do everything that might be desirable instantly, and impossible to select what comes first or should be postponed without some clear thinking-through of priorities.

» *Put some timing to it:* having established priorities you need to consider when things are to be done. What is urgent? What can be postponed without causing problems and what might be addressed in parts? (Perhaps something may be done early on, but action also planned to follow up and complete the training task later.)

» *Consider the method most suitable:* this needs to relate quite closely to timing. With a list of desirable development activities and priorities set, the next thing is to consider exactly how something will be approached (a course, a project, whatever).

» *Calculate costs:* this is always an important issue, and realistically may involve some compromise and balancing different approaches.

» *Link to an action plan:* the net result of these deliberations needs to be documented, and turned into a rolling plan that sets out what will be done, in what way, when and who will be involved.

In this kind of way training and development activities can be considered, worked out and scheduled on a basis that makes sense. Such consideration must:

» relate closely to operational matters; and
» link and liaise as necessary with any appropriate central department or manager (e.g. a training manager) – not least to draw on their experience and expertise.

Something like this may happen to you, indeed the better your manager the more likely it is to happen. The personal implications are clear, whatever management may do, you need to think things through in a similar way and you need a *written* plan – one that you can roll forward and fine-tune over time.

Starting from scratch this may take a moment. Keeping it up to date and monitoring progress need not take long (the plan might well be one sheet of paper, though make sure what you write is sufficient to make sense when looked at some months on). The process *is* manageable; certainly it is wholly in keeping with the results you will get from it.

THE METHODS

Many ways of undertaking some self-development activity are possible. They range from reading a book (you are under way already!) to studying for a qualification; more details in Chapter 6. First we consider only the main approaches that you can take:

» *Activity that occurs:* a host of things go on day by day that are part of or link to the development process. These include regular activities such as liaison with your manager, sales meetings and various kinds of evaluation including the ubiquitous annual job appraisal. They also include more ad hoc activity. For example, you may occasionally attend a formal course. Two things are important here. First, that you get the most from what goes on and integrate this into the entirety of your overall development. Secondly, you may want to take action to prompt your manager or organization to take more such action, indeed to try to secure specific initiatives that you feel will help you.

» *Your own activity:* this means activity that you instigate, personally and often privately. It might take advantage of company systems, say a library or resource center, or it might utilize outside resources or simply be something you can do on your own.

The task is to produce the best mix of activities you can that line up behind your own objectives. Some of these will certainly come in some way via your employer (if not are they the right employer?), others will come only after some liaison or persuasion – deploying some of your sales skill internally – and more may be necessary on your own initiative. The reality will always be a mix of some sort. Certainly you should avoid your development being short of what is needed because your only approach is to undertake what the organization makes available. It is your career, and ultimately the responsibility for it going well is with you.

THE RESULTS

Whatever activities you may undertake, and however they may be instigated, you want them to be useful. Overall there are four main ways in which development can help you.

» *In your current job:* the first level of benefit is in your current job. Development can provide help, for example by strengthening or adding skills to your armory, so that you can do it better. It can help you achieve better results – bearing in mind that even the best performance can be improved – and that in turn can be important to your future.

» *In future jobs:* success in your current job can, of course, help you towards new ones. In addition, development may look ahead, focusing for example on skills that, while not essential in the short term, are a prerequisite for promotion. Development helps make you promotable and puts you in a better position to make a career move when you want.

» *Increase your job rewards:* in sales work rewards can be closely linked to success and sales success is not difficult to measure. Remuneration is best viewed as a package: salary, commission, expenses, car, pension arrangements, bonuses, share schemes and so on. Progress in your job, driven by development, helps secure you the returns you want both in your current job and as you progress in your career.

» *Enhance your profile:* the perception of you within an organization is important. It may have intangible elements to it, but it is something real – are you seen as successful, as a high flyer, as someone having abilities beyond your current responsibilities? Because of what development can do, its results can improve the perception of you that exists within (and outside) the organization. This is a not insignificant benefit and one worth bearing in mind.

In addition, and of influence across the whole of your work and career, development influences job satisfaction. Whatever you want to do you probably want to enjoy it, to find it a challenge, to find it satisfying. However you define this for yourself, it is again worth bearing in mind. *You* make your career happen. Of course, many things influence it, but the job is to orchestrate the influences and make things go as far as possible the way you want. Aim high, and whatever else happens avoid being in a position where, if you pause to consider progress to date, your first comment begins: "If only I had . . . "

KEY LEARNING POINTS

» If you are to maximize your job performance, foster a successful career and make the progress you want, development, including that aspect of it on which you must be self-sufficient, is a vital activity.

» Development is something to which you must take an active approach. It must reflect real life and it must reflect an objective view of things. You may have weaknesses that you need to work to correct. You may have particular skills that you must add to your capabilities for the future. And certainly, like anyone in the dynamic area of sales, you have a continuing job to do just to keep up with the changing environment in which you work. Remember one of John Lennon's lines: "Life is what happens while you are busy making other plans." Time slips by all too fast and good intentions can remain just that. Development is not an option; it is a necessity. But it is something you can address and make successful. It helps you go where you want to go.

The Evolution of Self Development in Sales

This chapter examines the evolution of self development in sales and considers:

» the changing work environment;
» continuing professional development; and
» the future.

"God helps those who train themselves."

Lord Young of Graffham

Personally you may think of self development alongside the overall development – formal and informal – available within the organization that employs you. You will doubtless have wider objectives than those of the organization where, understandably, the focus is most likely to be on key results in your current job perhaps with half an eye on the longer-term (more than that in some organizations to be fair). In the broadest sense your need for self development is part of what has recently become known as the process of lifelong learning.

No one can rely on an expertise they may have remaining current forever. Indeed many people make far more changes during their career than was common years ago, and you may move into areas of work sufficiently different to necessitate a commensurately different portfolio of skills. How has this situation come about?

THE CHANGING WORK ENVIRONMENT

Numbers of changes have led to the current situation. Some affect the workplace generally as the following factors show.

» *Increasing number and importance of the "knowledge worker":* a trend in train that has been boosted since the computer revolution began in the 1950s and more and more people became employed in "knowledge" areas of work, rather than in manual tasks like production. White collar workers are now no longer any kind of elite and sales people along with many others are sometimes seen less as people and more as a resource: unless continual learning keeps them on top of their job, they cease to be as useful a resource and redundancy may follow.

» *Changing population:* it is well known that the population in many developed countries is aging. As we move ahead from the baby booms of the 1960s and mid 1970s companies will find the certain recruitment of new, younger people becomes more difficult. Already this is changing attitudes to training, which is seen as more necessary to keep older staff up to date. Training and development has perhaps always been seen as a good thing. If this situation continues then an individual must not be seen as being adverse to the process; indeed it has merit to develop one's own positive development attitude.

» *The IT revolution:* we are all very familiar with the fact and pace of change here (see also Chapter 4). You may be reading this having downloaded the text rather than buying the book, and in most sales jobs technological changes affect methods. The task is certainly not just talking to people any more – systems like CRM (customer relationship management) and the use of laptop computers during calls (for example, to show visuals or, linked to a telephone, check details back at the office) are routine. Certainly this aspect of the job demands regular updating and is something that self and more formal development must address regularly.

» *Increasing pressure for white-collar workers:* the workplace seems to put more pressure on people these days. People work longer hours, even on journeys to work using laptops and mobile telephones. They seem to be more stressed as more and more is apparently expected of them. Sales people are no exception to this. There is a danger that time for development will get squeezed out.

» *Increasing complexity:* many jobs, including sales, are more complex that they used to be. Technology adds an additional dimension and so do a multitude of other factors. Again training in all its forms is made more important.

» *The rise of the "gurus":* in the last 20, perhaps 30 years, there has been an increasing awareness of the need for all business processes – management, communications, the whole panoply of what makes organizations work – to be professional. As it has become recognized that no one is actually born with all the complex skills necessary to doing organizational jobs well, so development has become seen not as a luxury, but simply as a routine necessity of business life.

Other changes affect the sales area specifically.

» *Increased competition:* virtually whatever you sell, it will have more competitors than it did in the past, customers have more choice and are well aware of the fact. This affects the sales job directly. There is more information to learn, keep up to date with, and there are more sophisticated and precisely deployed approaches necessary. The essence of successful selling has become an ability to differentiate from competition.

» *Globalization:* the trend here is one part of what creates increased competitiveness. Whether it is because more and more business is done by multinational organizations, or the ability of smaller companies to transcend national boundaries (helped by such developments as the European Union) international competition continues to grow.

» *Product innovation:* more sophisticated products, largely another result of technological development, mean more to learn and discuss about them with customers. The major difference between say selling a fax machine and a complex integrated intranet system is clear.

» *More sophisticated (and wary) consumers:* training and the need for profitability has created a new breed of professional buyer. They are well informed, numerate and have high expectations. Selling must adapt to deal with them. In a different way customers have been, and are, regularly warned of the unscrupulous nature of sales people by examples of bad practice (such as pension mis-selling) and exposé-style consumer programs in the media.

» *Pressure on profitability:* competition and increasing costs seem to have brought margins under increasing pressure in recent year. This makes it more difficult to sell profitably and exaggerates the importance of ancillary skills such as negotiation.

» *Rising power of major customers:* another trend, greatest over the last 20 years, is that of the power held by large customers. This affects many industries; when products are sold to supermarkets, for example, the small number of massive retailers get control of most of the marketplace. Major customers are not just larger, they are different, they need different handling and different skills are necessary to do it well.

» *Reduced sales force size:* another result of higher costs is that the total cost of running a team of sales people has increased (costs include: salary, commission, travel costs, management, training and more). In turn the result of this is that sales teams have shrunk in size. With fewer people doing "bigger" jobs the effect on development is direct.

» *Technological change:* the IT revolution shows no sign of abating. While it continues it will affect sales jobs along with others and sales people will have to be able to blend traditional skills with new high-tech ones.

» *Time pressure:* this again is an overall trend, but sales people are affected and so are customers. The line between a customer seeing a sales person as providing a useful service and being a time waster is now a very fine one. If you cannot do the sales job – certainly run a sales meeting – in a time frame that is acceptable to your customers, you cannot do the job. Period.

In other words the sales job has changed. The title of an article in *Harvard Business Review* put it this way: "The salesman isn't dead, he's different". And one of the key ways in which it has changed is that it has become more challenging. No one in sales can afford to rest on their laurels and assume that today's techniques will be fine for the future. They will not. Ongoing, practical development is the order of the day. Those who succeed in future will only include those who embrace this idea. Formal development and self-development both have a role to play; together they can fit you for selling in the twenty first century.

CONTINUING PROFESSIONAL DEVELOPMENT

In the last 10 years or so the concept of continuing professional development (CPD) has spread widely in response to the kind of changes cataloged here, and the increased need for professionalism in many jobs. Initially limited to the professions (areas such as accountancy and law), CPD is now a regular feature of many people's lives.

» *Definition:* essentially CPD is a program of ongoing development undertaken as a mandatory part of someone's membership of a professional group. Activity is specified in broad detail, a set amount of time must be dedicated to it and records kept of exactly what has been done.

The requirements of professional bodies apart, such a scheme provides both added discipline to foster a commitment to ongoing self development and a mechanism to create the necessary continuity. Of course, what is done must be selected to make it genuinely useful (not just to clock up the necessary number of CPD points), if that is the case then such schemes are very valuable.

Some people are involved by virtue of their specialty. For example, accountancy needs selling just as much as anything else and if those doing this are qualified accountants, as many are, then they will automatically be part of such a scheme (for example, that run by the Institute of Chartered Accountants). More generally you may be interested in similar schemes closer to the actual business of selling. In the UK both the Chartered Institute of Marketing and The Institute of Professional Selling, which is linked to them, have CPD schemes. More about them appears in Chapter 9.

WHAT OF THE FUTURE?

The changes referred to are made. Waiting for "things to get back to normal" is simply not one of the options. Whichever way your career goes and whatever you do at present, it will change and change again.

> "For the company, to be agile is to be capable of operating profitably in a competitive environment of continually, and unpredictably changing customer opportunities. For an individual, to be agile is to be capable of contributing to the bottom line of a company that is constantly reorganizing its human and technological resources in response to unpredictably changing customer opportunities."
>
> *Roger N. Nagel, co-author of* Agile Competitors and Virtual Organizations

The word agility seems wholly appropriate to describe the key quality that must be brought to the workplace of the future. Certainly in the area of sales work this seems especially apposite. Looking back is only useful if it helps prepare you for the future. Gary Hamel said in summarizing the changed workplace "That was then, this is now." Though none of us can ever know exactly what circumstances we will face in the future, we can at least accept that change is the norm and act on that rather than ignoring or resenting it. There is no magic formula, but self development can certainly help you survive and prosper.

The E-Dimension

This chapter explores the e-dimension to self development under four main headings:

- » product changes;
- » business practice;
- » the sales process; and
- » the learning process.

"Business is about communications, sharing data and instanta-
neous decision making. If you have on your desk a device that
enables you to communicate and share data with your colleagues
around the world, you will have a strategic advantage."

Andrew S. Grove

As the quotation above makes clear information technology is having
a profound effect on business and how it works. In this chapter these
changes are commented upon under four main headings in terms of
how the IT revolution has affected products, business practices, the
sales process and the development and learning process.

PRODUCT CHANGES

The forward march of technology has spawned a whole raft of new
products and changed many more. It has also led to a situation where
some product life cycles become shorter and shorter as one new model
supersedes another, as is the case with computers, cameras and much
more. As a result more and more sales people are involved in selling
high tech items of various sorts.

In such areas the sales job has changed. It demands more knowledge
and skill to sell complex equipment rather than something essentially
straightforward. Those doing so may need to know *about* it, and be
able to demonstrate it; and do so in a way that makes it seem simple and
straightforward. Selling technology to people who struggle to understand it has become commonplace and it represents an opportunity.
People buy most readily from those who make such a process seem
straightforward – and safe. Clarity of explanation can be a powerful
tool here; it is not the easiest thing to do, however, and it must be got
right.

All in all the trends here are expanding many sales jobs. By definition
therefore they create an expanded need for development. Technical
and product knowledge must be just right, and there must be clear
understanding of how customers will use products if explanation is to
be well matched to customer needs.

The IT revolution means that sales people selling high tech products
have more to learn, more complex things to learn, and a heightened
need to keep their knowledge and skills up to date – apparently at a

faster and faster pace. Anyone involved in this sort of scenario will need to look at their development plans accordingly.

BUSINESS PRACTICE

Here too a plethora of changes are in train, with no doubt more to come. Even simple examples make the point.

» Electronic equipment at cash points not only completes a sales transaction, it gathers information about consumers and links to stock control. Anyone selling to such stores faces people with detailed information about the sale of their product.
» The new additional purchase possibilities of the Internet are changing some business areas. For instance you might have bought this text in book form from a retail bookshop, or electronically from an organization like Amazon. Certainly the existence of Amazon means book publishers have a new kind of outlet to sell to and it changes the attitudes of those buying for retailers.
» Websites have changed forever the way people can access information with it now being quicker and easier to research things than ever before. Amongst other things this means that someone selling had better expect that their prospects and customers will be better informed than ever before. For example, they are likely to have up to date information about many aspects of your competitors' offerings. Their existing image of your own organization may be influenced in a similar way (if your organization has a Website, it is only sensible to keep up to date with what it says).

In addition, it may behove a seller to understand and appreciate something of the problems that their customers face in adopting and implementing new, higher tech processes. While there are undoubted benefits from many such changes, the process of making the change can be painful.

Again there are areas here that development should sensibly address.

THE SALES PROCESS

Sales people are increasingly using a barrage of technology in the course of their jobs. Some, like the mobile phone, are comparatively straightforward, very useful and now ubiquitous. Others present a learning curve, sometimes one that seems endless. A laptop computer is now routinely used at sales meetings (to check stock or delivery times, for instance, or show visuals to customers) for everything from placing an order to completing customer records. Some of these systems are not complicated; others may have many elements to them and become a major part of the job. So-called customer relationship management (CRM) systems used particularly to assist the interface with major customers are important. Anyone who struggles with them, or whose productivity is reduced by slowness in using them, is at a disadvantage.

An important point needs to be made here. The job is not just to be able to utilize the new technology in a sales context, rather it is to do so in a way that customers like, appreciate and find useful. Just because something is technically possible does not mean that it is going to set customers alight; it may just rub them up the wrong way. For example, after my telephone and myself were tied up for an hour and twenty minutes as a company's electronic brochure downloaded it, I was much less inclined to do business with them. And this despite the quality of what I then had in front of me.

Nevertheless most sales people are faced with electronic systems in their own organization and those of their customers; there is a lot to learn and a lot of subsequent change to keep up with in this area.

THE LEARNING PROCESS

Developments in IT are not doing away with traditional learning and training methods entirely, well not often. Rather they are enhancing the range of options and extending what is possible and how and when time can be spent on development. The terminology is somewhat loose, however, with some overlaps. The main methods to be aware of are:

» *Open (or distance) learning:* this is the modern version of the old correspondence course (still itself alive and well). The "package" presents material in a range of forms: manuals and books, CDs, CD-ROMs, DVDs, videos, even telephone or Internet. A course is self-administered, and takes place wherever and whenever the trainee wants. The site may vary, for example some work being done at a computer and some not. Distance learning invariably involves two further things:

> » individual work projects and exercises; and
> » interaction with a central tutor of some sort, so that an element of measurement and counseling is also involved (this can take place through a variety of forms of communication from e-mail to face-to-face contact).

» *Programmed learning:* this both predates open learning and can be part of it. The original form was a manual, now it is more likely to be computer based. In essence it is a form of training that checks progress. It presents a lesson, then a test, and the next lesson (which may recap) reflects the result of the test.

» *Computer assisted training (CAT):* this is simply training taken "on screen." It can include elements of programmed learning. It can be a long course, taken in parts, or constitute only one discreet session. Some ongoing training is delivered regularly by such means (for instance, updating of product knowledge). But here what characterizes the method is that the computer element is only part of the total experience. A trainer is also involved and the complete course may include a variety of other methodologies.

» *Computer based training (CBT):* here the method is solely computer based. The mix of methods used may again vary: there may be little more than text on screen or it may involve the many elements of more sophisticated distance learning. In some instances set up involves inserting a disk, in others material is downloaded from the Internet or an organization's own intranet.

However, the variety here makes summary impossible. The following are the key variables.

» *The time a program takes to go through:* this can vary literally from a few minutes to several months or years.

» *The quality that is inherent in the program:* just because it is high-tech does not guarantee good quality or ease of learning.

» *The match of methodology and topic:* the method must suit the content. For example, it is fine to present knowledge-imparting factual programs on product knowledge or associated information (for instance, medical facts for those selling pharmaceutical products) straight from system to trainee. Interactive skills – like selling – benefit from a more interactive approach. There is a danger of things learnt by rote being deployed in the same way; and selling is conspicuously not like that.

» *The people doing the learning:* for example, at this stage of IT development there are those who turn automatically to their computer screen, and work comfortably from it, and those who dread it, believing it is awkward and preferring to pick up a book. There is a way to go before any one technology, never mind any one system, holds sway.

The traditionalists will hanker after and promote standard training methodology from workshops to role-play for a while longer. The innovators will grasp at every new solution and seek out technological ways of tackling every learning experience. So be it. Realistically we will all be faced with a mixture of methods for a while longer, and often with the job of selecting from competing methodologies when faced with deciding how to tackle a particular learning task.

Perhaps this is a good thing. Effective learning benefits from variety, as it also does to a degree from repetition (so see the video *and* read the book). The combination of trainer-led and interactive methods alongside many more modern methods, certainly over the long term, is the reality for most people. In selling you have to consider what is available and take the best of it, bearing in mind that you will probably never find the time for everything you want to do and find out about.

Bear in mind that sometimes the relationship between method and content and the significance of a particular thing is not always clear. Sometimes it is the small things, an e-mail from a manager or mentor (IT even makes mentoring more productive and easier to undertake) that have the most positive impact when implemented. Some technological solutions are designed to reflect that fact (for example, a California-based training provider offers a "three minute sales course", providing three minutes of stimulation and learning on a daily basis – www.genie@influence-integrity.com for more details). Who can honestly say they cannot find three minutes a day, provided they gained from it?

Similarly, lower tech methods that link well to the particular nature of the sales job will remain in use and continue to be useful. An example here is the simple cassette tape (or perhaps CD). This can usefully be listened to during the many hours sales people spend driving. It may not be high-tech, but it suits.

THE CORPORATE UNIVERSITY

A resource center is akin to a library. A "corporate university" is more. The report "The future of corporate learning", published in 2000 by the Department of Trade and Industry, Henley Management College, defines it thus:

> "A corporate university is formed when a corporation seeks to relate its training and development strategies to its business strategies by co-ordination and integration and by development of intellectual capital within the organization in pursuit of its corporate aims and objectives."

Why does it seem compulsory in such reports to write long complicated sentences without even a comma ... sorry, I digress. The point is that large organizations, or some of them, see providing ongoing training as requiring significant investment. They aim to provide a complete development resource in whatever form makes best sense for people and for the achievement of training objectives.

Not all new technology is good, certainly no one methodology has a monopoly on the best way forward. It is horses for courses. The large organization may not get everything right, but at least a wide variety of things are available and new ways of doing things are tested. If you work for such an organization, and the report quotes organizations as different as Motorola and Ernst & Young (which operate a "virtual business school") as taking this approach then you have the opportunity to take advantage of what is on offer. The key is flexibility. Dr John O'Connor at Motorola says:

> "People in the telecommunications business need knowledge on several levels, including technical know-how, product specific knowledge and competitive intelligence. Each of these requires a dynamic and evolving educational framework. The classroom model cannot efficiently deliver for large, disparate population

groups. Motorolans need information that is relevant, up to date, on time and in manageable chunks. Learning technologies can play a strong part in making this scenario successful.''

Not surprising that this company has for long been regarded as a leader in this kind of attitude and action in training. That said, Dr O'Connor regards the future as being one in which e-learning will be "self-directed within a disciplined framework." In other words technology can help, especially if well orchestrated by an organization at pains to promote learning. But whatever may be offered, the individual must act to seek what is best for them. Much of the initiative in the future will need to be individual and personal. Every little initiative taken can help; the process is cumulative. To quote Dr O'Connor again: "Many people will look for five-minute learning interventions."

The culture of an organization affects how they set up any such scheme. It is clearly there to advance people's learning and thus their effectiveness. Additionally it may have other roles. For example, the university in Barclays Bank allows training or development activities completely outside the business arena to receive some financial help. Maybe this allows unusual links to be made with work skills; certainly it must be motivational.

So, make no mistake, even in a large company, it will not all be done for you (though many resources may well be on tap). In a context of smaller companies you may need to look outside, to a professional or educational body, to a trade organization or even to a friendly business library. The latter may need to be something you visit regularly if you are to make your own ongoing self-development work effective and keep yourself not just up to date, but ahead of the game.

Reviewing the ongoing changes in this field in his book *The E-Learning Revolution*, Martyn Sloman says simply that: "the challenge is to put the focus on the learners." However much your own employer is tied up in this revolution, you need to keep abreast of the developments and seize any opportunity to include appropriate new technology in the development methods you decide to use. The key questions are – what works and what helps you?

The Global Dimension in Self Development for Sales People

This chapter considers what increasing globalization can mean for you and how you can develop your sales job and make it successful.

"... today, thousands of competitors from every corner of the world are able to serve customers well. To develop effective strategy, we as leaders have to understand what's happening in the rest of the world, to reshape our organization and respond accordingly. No leader can hope to guide an enterprise into the future without understanding the commercial, political and social impact of the global economy."

Kenichi Ohmae, McKinsey Tokyo

The fact that the global market influences local ones hardly needs mentioning these days. Most people in selling face international competitors. The signs of multinational brands are all around us. And the inter-connectedness of everything in the business world means that far-flung events are as likely as any other to influence success at a local level. The details of all this are beyond our brief here, though other volumes in this series, including *Global Marketing* and *Global Organization,* bear testimony to the trends and the importance of them.

Here the focus is much more personal. What does this increasing global influence mean for you and how you can develop your sales job and make it successful?

A RANGE OF WORK OPPORTUNITIES

First, you may want to consider international opportunities as an element of your own career goals. The following may constitute major career moves, but they might also be undertaken on a temporary basis or as a minor part of your overall work portfolio for specific developmental advantage.

» *Work for a multinational company:* if it suits you, then being in a multinational automatically extends the possibilities open to you. You have networking opportunities on a broader scale and may also have opportunities to relocate abroad on some basis (more on both of these possibilities anon).

» *Locate overseas:* a spell working overseas may demand some development to fit you for it. You may or may not see a spell in the Netherlands or New Zealand as a start of a lifetime there, or a lifetime in a variety of overseas locations, but you are certainly going to learn from it even in the short term. Myles Proudfoot, who was moved by Procter & Gamble from the UK to corporate headquarters in Cincinnati says: " The network of contacts I have developed and wide exposure to new people is helping me to connect with the latest ideas and opportunities . . . it has changed the way I see the business world, exposed me to new horizons and raised my expectations of what I want to do in the future" (a fuller quote appears in the *ExpressExec* title *Career Management*). He has had to adapt and adapt fast, but is learning a great deal too. Already new responsibilities are involving him further in the international dimensions of the business and as I write this he is traveling to Australia and Singapore.

» *Work in exporting:* this is a particular field of selling, but it is one that normally gets you traveling and puts you in touch with people and organizations that may help your development plans. Although not for everyone, this is the kind of thing that well illustrates long-term development and progress. For example, you may want to work overseas so a spell in exporting may be a step in the right direction. It may also be one that justifies language training so that at some future date your learning and experience allow you to add "fluent in French and German" to your résumé.

» *Include an overseas travel element within your job:* all sorts of things might see you making trips overseas – and developing contacts and learning opportunities as you do so. Some things need nurturing. Can you be the company's representative on an international committee, the nominated attendee at an exhibition, or the person that briefs people at the overseas end of a new collaboration? My own work has involved a good deal of travel over the years, and I remember that the first time I ever went overseas was to a conference in France. Over time I have learnt a great deal from acquiring something of an international perspective. This has helped directly with my work and added an enjoyable dimension to what I do. Even seemingly small things can be valuable. Attending an event in the States this year – the annual conference of the American Society of Training and Development – I was amazed at how much information and how many contacts could be accessed in just two days (a couple of further days exploring New Orleans where it was held was fun too). For some readers this may be an area to start to work on.

A key element about all of this is people. Having a wide range of contacts is always likely to benefit your development, as you can learn so much from others, and ensuring some of them are overseas broadens the effect still more.

INTERNATIONAL NETWORKING

Networking is a well-established process these days. The old saying has it: "It is not what you know, it is who you know that matters" and of course networking can assist business directly. It can assist career progress – and it can assist learning. Here we are concerned about the international dimension of self-development. You may well want to organize, and interact with an international network of contacts. Ask questions – do you have anyone in the office there that knows about X? Work from one person to the next and keep in touch with those that seem, or prove, useful.

If you have an international element to your job this may act to direct it. If not there may still be merit in looking further a field. Start at home as it were, and work your way out. Make use of links that exist even if you are not involved in them. If your company has an office or a distributor in a foreign city get the contact name. This may not be the one you ultimately want but they may lead you to it.

EXAMPLE

Perhaps I can illustrate this principle with a personal example. I work regularly in South East Asia. One contact I have established in Singapore, a local consultant called Gary Lim, provides a classic example of long-distance networking. Of course, we meet occasionally, and he's an excellent guide to local eating. But more often contact is via e-mail and the occasional posted item.

Through him I can:

» obtain support and assistance of many sorts (for example, he once got a prompt payment from what looked like being a bad debtor by making a single phone call);
» extend my range of contacts by linking to others he knows;

» check the local view on something (economic, cultural or whatever);

» find a sounding board for ideas or to check something factual; and

» discover other sources of information and advice (from a local library to a Website in China).

And more besides – many of these contacts I learn from. It is also an interesting and pleasant contact (he's a nice guy!). As I said to another colleague the other day "Everyone should have a Gary in every overseas location that's important to them". I hope he finds his link with me useful also.

Of course the people you link up with need to be tailored to your situation and your needs. Remember networking is a two-way process, you get out what you put in, but it is also a very constructive one and should be part of anyone's self-development activity.

Most organizations have a variety of training resources. Being in close touch with different organizations from your own, even a subsidiary with strong links to the principal, can double the material to which you have access. Besides you can meet some good people along the way.

CULTURAL DEVELOPMENT

Here let us focus on the skills directly associated with selling for a moment. Selling is only a particular form of communication. Certainly it is dependent on the ability to be clear and achieve understanding and to describe things in a way that brings them to life. You can be expert in selling only if you are able to direct it towards specific objectives and to deploy just the right combination of approaches to make it work in each individual case you address. Not least this is because customers want a tailored approach; conversely they do not want to hear a standardized approach. They are individuals and want to be treated as such.

International sales bring an additional dimension to the communications involved. Cultural differences are important, and an aspect of learning if you are going to be involved with international business consists of getting to know something about them. This may be another goal for self development.

You may need to learn a foreign language – even brief visits (on which there might well be a good deal hanging in sales) necessitate some local knowledge. This can come in a variety of ways: reading (*The Cultural Gaffs Pocketbook,* Angelena Boden, Management Pocketbooks, is a good and succinct starting point), networking, or talking to an organization such as a chamber of commerce within which someone knows the area. Time spent in reconnaissance is seldom wasted, it is said, and if you do not want to offend a Buddhist by pointing your feet at them, be thought pushy by smiling too soon at a Korean, or mistake a Bulgarian nod for agreement (it means the reverse) then it is good advice.

If your job or career depends on extensive or important dealings with any particular culture or country, then this advice should be taken very seriously. Much will still depend on experience, so make sure too that you learn the lessons on your early visits to another country.

INTERNATIONAL SOURCES OF DEVELOPMENT

You may want to source some of what you take on board during your self development from outside the country, indeed this may be the best way to access certain information and keep up to date. This includes information about products, competitors and customers.

Some of this information is transient, but if it helps you conduct just one sales meeting better then the activity qualifies as development. For example, a delegate on a course I was conducting recently in the UK told me that he sold to a multinational. He looked up a Website maintained by the parent company in the States and was able to quote things (the information was apparently not readily available in the UK) at a meeting that made him appear very thorough in his research and up to date with his facts. This enabled him to give an impression that "certainly helped win the business."

Many different kinds of source can be used.

» Professional and trade organizations
» Trade and professional magazines

» Websites
» Individual companies
» Educational bodies (for example, a university or college)
» Newsletters
» Training bodies and organizations . . . and more.

This sort of initiative can be developed around your situation and interests; and around what is convenient – for example you may have no time to source an overseas journal from a library, but can download features from it electronically. Subscribing (and, yes, you may have to pay for it) to just one journal from overseas might give you information that none of your competitors has (or your peers either, if you take a competitive view on that).

BEST PRACTICE

If you work for a large company some of the training provided may be made available on an international basis. Doing this may create significant projects. If you are in regular touch with your training and HR people (see Chapter 6), you may even get advance warning of this; if so there may be merit in trying to organize to get involved in the early stages. Such a project is best described through an example.

EXAMPLE – PRODUCT TRAINING AT CABLE & WIRELESS

Cable & Wireless is a major global telecoms organization and operates in more than 70 countries. Their regional division has activities especially well spread with operations current in markets as diverse and far-flung as the Solomon Islands and the West Indies. On launching a range of new Internet products there was a need to ensure that members of the widely dispersed sales team understood them sufficiently well to do justice to selling them, indeed to get the launch off to a good start.

It was decided to put the information over through specially designed e-learning (designed by Fuel, a London-based specialist training company). The training addressed the basic technical knowledge that sales people needed together with knowledge of the benefits and how to put them over to customers. The approach was designed to be lively and visual (for example, equating networks to traffic and motorway junctions). After a pilot scheme, it was made available to some 1400 staff, 94 per cent of whom reported favorably on both method and content.

Several points seem inherent here. First, it is good to see a company rating the importance of product knowledge so highly. Secondly, one presumes that this approach assisted the product launch to a considerable extent; one imagines it would have been a slower and less certain process if a trainer had to travel the world conducting endless courses. Clearly the material itself must be well designed for this sort of thing to work well.

One other thing that focuses on the individual trainees: they had to take it seriously and actually go through the material (many things probably affected this in this case, from the punchy e-mails that announced the initiative to the prevailing state of motivation at the time). For the dedicated self developer the moral is clear. If good material is made available by your organization, even from the other side of the world, always take it seriously. Make the time to use it properly and engage in any feedback that it involves.

Selling is never easy; it makes no sense to try to undertake it less well informed than is necessary – and effectively fighting competition with one arm tied behind your back.

Finally, it is now routine to be able to tap into information from a plethora of sources using the world wide Web (see Chapter 4).

Next we review the main types of methodology in Chapter 6.

''There are no national frontiers to learning.''

Japanese proverb

The State of the Art

This chapter considers what sales people actually do and how they do it in the context of an open-ended and ongoing process of self development.

"A little knowledge that acts is worth infinitely more than much knowledge that is idle."

Kahil Gibran

This is the chapter in which the "what you do" and "how you do it" of self development for sales people is examined. There is no magic formula, many different things can contribute to successful self development and it is in deciding on the mix of what you do that you first influence your ultimate success.

THINKING ABOUT DEVELOPMENT

Remember that development can only ever do three things:

» *impart knowledge:* so you can learn about business practices and sales techniques and about your product (the ubiquitous product knowledge), markets, customers, competitors and any technical background that working in a particular area makes necessary;
» *develop skills:* introducing you to new skills, maintaining, improving or refining your abilities in everything from core sales techniques to specialist computer skills you may need to deploy; and
» *change attitudes:* study can change the way you think about things, although this may take longer than adopting some new skills. For example, something like managing your time effectively is as much a question of the attitude you take to it (and the habits this develops) as to slavishly following techniques.

Next, if your development is going to change anything, two other things are key.

» You have to set aside some *time* for self development. This need not be excessive or unmanageable, but it needs to be there and it needs to be made available on a regular basis.
» *Application* is equally important. There is all the difference in the world between skimming through a book, to take a simple example, so that you can say that you have done so, and reading it carefully, studying it over a little longer period, making some notes and perhaps also resolving to take some action as a result.

Given that self development has immediate and longer-term objectives, you need to consider both. This means:

» analysis of the development gap (in line with what was said in Chapter 2) to ascertain what specific areas need addressing, how urgently and with what priority; and
» looking at the development gap with the long term especially in mind: you need to consider self development in context of your overall career intentions – and you must be wholly clear what these are.

So, consider next the overall approach that active career management suggests.

ANALYZING YOUR CAREER INTENTIONS

There is a danger that good intentions will direct you towards any possible development activity. With time necessarily limited, you have to be sure that any development activity to which you subscribe is accurately lined up behind your intentions and likely to make a difference in the way you want.

So, what thinking should you apply to ensure that your self-development will be well focused on clear career intentions? Logically you need to address your skills, work values, and personal – and non-work – characteristics, alongside the market and the potential rewards. You then need to consider how all this relates to your "ideal job" and the real possibilities in the real world. The details of how this thinking can proceed appear in the boxed paragraph (adapted from my *ExpressExec* title, *Career Management*).

ANALYSIS ON WHICH TO BASE CAREER INTENTIONS

There are several stages of thinking that are useful.

Assess your skills

You may be surprised how many you have including, for example:

» Communicating
» Influencing

» Managing (people or projects)
» Problem solving
» Creativity
» Social skills
» Numeracy
» Special skills (everything from languages to computer usage).

Assess your work values

Here you should consider factors such as having:

» A strong need to achieve
» A need for a high salary
» High job satisfaction requirements
» A liking for doing something "worthwhile"
» A desire to be creative.

There may be many other factors here from wanting to see travel opportunities to being independent in the way you work or operating as part of a team.

Assess your personal characteristics

Here you consider such factors as whether you are a:

» Risk taker
» An innovator
» Someone who can work under pressure
» A perfectionist.

Consider what kind of person you are and how these characteristics affect your work situation.

Assess your non-work characteristics

Consider such factors as:

» Family commitments
» Where you want to live
» How much time you are happy to spend away from home

» Social patterns
» Outside interests.

Time is the crucial factor here, together with the kind of balance you see as necessary for you between work and non-work elements of life.

Match your analysis to the market demands

In other words consider how well your overall capabilities and characteristics fit current market opportunities. This avoids you seeking out a route that is doomed before it starts. If anything to do with computers, say, throws you, then you either have to learn to cope with it, or avoid areas of work dependent on a high degree of computer literacy. While you need to acknowledge what you want, and would be unhappy without, you also need a measure of hard-nosed realism in considering this.

Consider the picture so far alongside rewards

This may have come up along the way, but is worth separate consideration and it may be worth reviewing your attitude to different elements of the remuneration package separately. Consider such items as salary, bonuses, profit share, share schemes, cars and specific perks. (I wonder how many people work for banks because of the special mortgage loans they often give?)

With all the information and feelings that the analysis so far will engender you can now move on to phase two. The first thing to consider here is what would be the best working situation.

Your ideal job

Here consider such things as your preferred:

» Area of work – tasks, responsibilities etc.
» People situation – many/few, managing others, in a team etc.
» Working environment – large or small organization, big city location etc.
» Home location – and its location relative to work
» Rewards.

Note: if, at this point you are undecided as to what is an ideal job, you may want to consider formal career guidance. There are agencies that are very helpful, and psychometric tests that can show what would suit you with some real accuracy. This is something you may want to investigate further.

Match your ideal with the market possibilities

Here you may have difficult decisions to make in matching your wishes, your strengths and the real possibilities in the market. On the one hand it is good to aim high, on the other you may waste time and effort on something that can never be achieved. Not easy, but it is wise advice never to cut off options for no good reason. There is no reason why a more far out goal cannot be kept on the back burner in case it becomes more achievable in the future.

CLEAR OBJECTIVES

The most important thing that this analysis allows you to do is to set clear objectives: and this means objectives that are *specific, measurable and timed*. They have to assist you in a directional sense. If you say simply "I want to earn lots of money" this does not set out a route to help you to do so. Treat objectives as desirable results (I plan to earn X amount by the age of 35, or I plan to develop negotiating skills that are a match for even a major customer). Then you have a chance to match clear objectives with a clear and workable plan to help you get to them. Aim high by all means, but make sure objectives are essentially achievable.

If you are already on a sales-orientated career path some of these decisions may already have been made. It can be easy to overlook things, however, and assume that too many things that in fact demand a decision are fixed when they are not. Careful consideration is always to be recommended. You may need to undertake some research too to make sure all this is factually based (for example, referring to salary surveys).

Knowing exactly what you are aiming at, from the point of view of both job and career, you can now plan and implement some self-development activity.

THE NEXT JOB

You can do worse than focus carefully and closely on any "next job" you have in mind. This may be something you want in its own right, or it may unashamedly be a stepping-stone to further moves. In either case you need to be sure that you are equipped specifically for it. Sales management makes a good example. The skills required to do a good sales job certainly help in management, and a sales manager is likely to go on doing some selling and certainly needs to be good at it. But management demands additional skills. (Figure 6.1 highlights this (and another ExpressExec title is *Sales Management*). It is perfectly possible for someone who is an excellent sales person to be promoted (in part because of that excellence no doubt), and yet prove to lack the necessary skills to make a good sales manager. Look at what is needed and work to equip yourself to be able to do the job you aspire to.

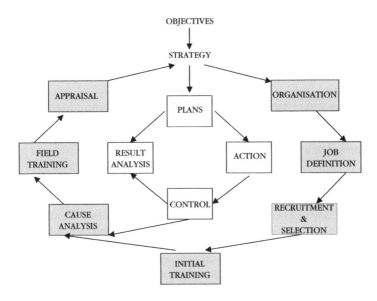

Fig. 6.1 The main responsibilities of the sales management job.

Figure 6.1 shows the main responsibilities of the sales management job. The inner circle illustrates those tasks that are essentially short-term, and the outer incorporates the longer-term.

AN ACTION PLAN

Again this was mentioned in Chapter 2, but it stands emphasis. You need a written plan. This need not be voluminous. It might only be a couple of sheets of A4 paper, perhaps linked to a simple year planner (the sort of thing that comes with a Filofax style diary system is ideal); or it might be a screen or two on your computer or electronic personal organizer.

This can specify what you will do, when you will do it and the method(s) to be used.

Sometimes it may be specific: "Attend presentation skills course 20/21 June". On other occasions it may be only a guide. For example, specifying that you will read a particular book "during August". Over the short-term the plan should be more specific than the long term; however the planning process rolls on and things can be firmed up as time passes. You should use the plan to record the full implications involved. For instance, what do you want to do after attending a presentations skills course, make more presentations or get someone to critique the next one you make? Line up whatever sequence of events makes sense. If you ensure that when a moment is passed it records accurately what you did, then it will create a useful record.

Now, what are the options? What is the kind of things that you can do and how do you decide what is best?

Selecting methods

Perhaps the first thing to address here is some guidelines on assessing the relative merits of different methods. Without thinking about this in the right way, there is a danger that you will always select whatever seems "easiest," and this may not give you the best results.

Choice of method must blend, and sometimes compromise, between a number of key factors which include what is most:

» *effective* (and will be most likely to ensure that learning does take place);
» *productive* (and will make the best use of time);
» *convenient* (which includes what you are best set up to do, and how much something will disrupt operational matters – or not);
» *interesting* (motivation is always an important side effect of development, something management should keep an eye on – certainly you will want the process to be as stimulating as possible);
» *timely* (in the sense of both when the development, or the result of it, is needed and in terms of fitting in with other operational considerations of timing);
» *fitting* (that is what fits best into the continuum of other, and ongoing, training and development either that you plan or that you are required to do);
» *well-tailored* (to what you want to achieve and the prevailing circumstances); and
» *financially suitable* (not necessarily the cheapest way of doing something, but always it must be possible to justify the costs – especially if you are financing it yourself). Note that if you regard the return as sufficiently important, while you may always want to start by asking your employer to fund anything you want to do, there may be some things worth personal expenditure. If you do this remember to keep records and receipts, as you may well be able to claim such costs against tax.

Choice of method has the overall intention of making the process both effective and productive. Some methods are not mutually exclusive and you may want to do a number of things in combination or in sequence, coming at something from a variety of directions. Simple methods may act in their own right or be an inherent part of a larger event as, for example, reading a book may be a preliminary to attending a course.

As has already been said, many ideas and approaches that qualify as methods are extremely simple. Others are more complex and time consuming, and realistically what is needed is a mix.

USEFUL PEOPLE

Many different people may be able to help in your self development. We will start with comment about one resource everyone but the self-employed has, and which can assist development: the boss.

The learning manager

If the term "learning organization" can be used (it is: it means an organization that encourages ongoing learning and acts to make it possible), then the term learning manager makes similar sense. Surveys show that at the very top of the qualities that people look for in a boss is "someone I learn from." A good manager can be your single most important spur to development. (If yours is the very reverse then it needs thinking about: are you going to succeed in such a circumstance? It may affect your future.) A good manager will consider development important, they will recognize that it serves a positive purpose (not just addressing weaknesses), and will work with their people to identify and close any development gap.

Realistically, you thus have two routes to obtaining assistance from your manager:

» taking advantage of the things they offer; and
» encouraging – and sometimes persuading – them to do more or let you do more. We will take this as read as we review developmental methods later.

Your manager stands or falls on your performance, and those of others who report to them. They have a vested interest in your doing well and in helping you do just that. In the sales role there are certainly things that should happen and which you can use to your developmental advantage, for example things that occur – or which you might prompt – at sales meetings (more details appear in Chapter 7).

Whatever you may learn from your own manager, there are other people who can help too. Some can do so on a regular basis, a process called mentoring.

Mentors

A mentor is someone who exercises a low-key and informal developmental role. More than one person can be involved in the mentoring of a single individual and, while what they do is akin to some of the things a line manager should do, more typically in terms of how the word is used a mentor is specifically *not* your line manager. It might be someone more senior, someone on the same level or from elsewhere in the organization. An effective mentor can be a powerful force in your development. So how do you get yourself a mentor?

In some organizations this is a regular part of ongoing development. You may be allocated one or able to request one. Equally you may need to act to create a mentoring relationship. You can suggest it to your manager, or direct to someone you think might undertake the role, and take the initiative.

What makes a good mentor? The person must have authority (this might mean they were senior, or just that they were capable and confident). They should have suitable knowledge, experience, counseling skills, appropriate clout and a willingness to spend some time with you (their doing this with others may be a positive sign). Finding that time may be a challenge. One way to minimize that problem is to organize mentoring on a swap basis: someone agrees to help you and you line up your own manager to help them, or one of their people.

Then a series of informal meetings can result, together creating a thread of activity through the operational activity. These meetings need an agenda, but more importantly they need to be constructive. If they are, then one thing will naturally lead to another and a variety of occasions can be utilized to maintain the dialog. A meeting followed by a brief encounter as people pass on the stairs; a project and a promise to spend a moment on feedback; an e-mail or two passing in different directions; all may contribute. What makes this process useful is the commitment and quality of the mentor. Where such relationships can be set up, and where they work well, they add a powerful dimension to the ongoing cycle of development, one that it is difficult to imagine being bettered in any other way.

Overall, what you learn from the ongoing interactions and communications you have with your line manager and others can be invaluable.

It may leave some matters to be coped with in other ways, but it can prove the best way to cope with many matters and also to add useful reinforcement in areas of development that also need a more formal approach. As both parties become familiar with the arrangement, and with each other, it can become highly productive. Having been lucky enough to have someone in this role myself for many years I know that sometime just a few minutes spent together can crack a problem or lead to a new initiative.

Note: a mentor is usually taken to be someone senior to the person to whom they act as mentor. But a similar relationship is possible with colleagues (for example, other members of your sales team). There is no reason why you cannot forge a number of useful and reciprocal alliances, perhaps each designed to help in rather different ways.

NETWORKING

Your line manager and anyone in a mentoring role are obviously prime contacts. Beyond that you should keep in touch with people, other than your manager, who may be able to assist your development. There may be a variety of them. Such may include your manager's manager, a company training manager and others in human resources (HR), the personnel manager, technical people (if you sell a technical product your product knowledge may be improved simply by meeting regularly and informally with a contact in a technical role), and whoever may run any resource center the company may maintain.

The other key liaison to run is with colleagues. If you work in a sales team you may be separated geographically; however where territories touch then regular meetings may be possible (for example on North and South London territories). It may be useful simply at the level of having a sounding board, and a companion for lunch. Differences of experience, skill or outlook could make it much more creative.

DEVELOPMENT METHODS

Key personal relationships apart, there are, as has been said, many things you can do; to start, we review the classic course - something that comes in a surprising variety of guises.

Courses, and more courses

There are all sorts of learning events and the terminology is less than exact. There are courses, seminars, meetings, workshops, conferences and more. In considering what to do an assessment has to be made of the options.

You may be sent on courses, but you may also want to request attendance. Any course you pick must reflect your overall intentions and objectives; then – our concern here – the question is which course to select? Answering this question is not a science, and judgment and preference play a key part. Some juggling of disparate factors may be necessary, and the following are designed to help cut through the plethora of alternatives and assist some sensible decision-making.

» *How long?* Usually this is a compromise between what the content demands, the level of participation and the realism of time away from the job.
» *Internal or external?* Various factors are important here: would it be useful to get an outside perspective? To mix with others? What about timing? What internal resources exist?
» *Which trainer?* You may feel a "personality style" external event is best, or have preferences regarding which of a number of internal trainers or consultants you feel would be most useful.
» *What format?* Here there are many options, from a short session of a few hours to long courses; not least you must be realistic about how long you are likely to get agreement to be away from the job.
» *How much participation?* This is not just a question of what would be most satisfying, but of what the topic needs, the number of participants etc.
» *The devil you know?* All things being equal, it may make sense to stick with a trainer or style of training that you have used in the past, and therefore know. This can lead to messages building logically one on another.
» *Management preference?* Here you need to consider what will be most likely to be approved – does the company only like things that have an entirely practical focus or are they inclined to experiment?

Overall there is another factor, always important, that of cost. While poor training may be worse than none at all, one has to be realistic and cost is a factor that dictates, at least in part, what decisions are taken. Again you need to be realistic, it might be better not ask to go on a month's training three months into a new appointment, for instance.

Getting the best from course attendance

Whatever course is selected, you want to get the best from it. Two factors are important here:

» *Pre-course briefing:* whether you have been involved in the choice to attend a particular course or not, you need to be clear why you are attending and what should come from it. It is well worth the few minutes it takes to sit down with someone – your own manager or a central training person – to go through this. You should be clear what the objectives of a course are, and its limitations – it may only address part of something you ultimately want to deal with comprehensively. Such a briefing will help you to go with clear and specific personal objectives in mind. Such briefing and thinking sets up attendance so that its effectiveness is maximized.

» *Behavior on the program:* these days it is unlikely you will find yourself on a course you regard as useless. Even if you approach a course positively, however, you need to maximize the benefit of your attendance on it. After all, once it is over any action may be more difficult. Certainly, on a short course attention given literally to the process of attending is worthwhile. So check out objectives, make a note of issues or problems you want to raise and generally think about how you can make attending a worthwhile experience (see Chapter 7 for more details).

Activity courses

One special form of course is worth a mention also. Imagine that a cold and wet landscape stretches away into the mist and you know the nearest cup of tea and warm bath is miles distant. You and assorted colleagues are huddled under the dripping branches of a tree. On the ground nearby are three old car tires, some lengths of rope, six planks of wood and a pink cushion. How do you turn all that into something that floats, gets you across the river and ... where actually is the river? The "outward bound" type of course is loved and hated in equal measure.

Some people swear they are the ultimate developer of leadership skills or teamwork. Some just swear. Certainly their use needs care. Not every provider of such things is equally good; some are good at providing a physical challenge, but less good at relating it in any meaningful way to the work place. Not every group is suited to this sort of thing, and certainly someone less physically able or adept might find tagging along after their more athletic team mates taught them nothing but resentment.

That said, they seem to suit the culture of some organizations and, if they do, they provide a different way of approaching certain training tasks. They are almost certain to get the undivided attention of the group for a while; it is pretty difficult to worry about immediate operational problems when you are high in the air dangling on the end of a rope over mud of indeterminate depth. They can be fun but, if you find yourself going on one, the question of briefing is doubly important. If it is not clear what you should get from it – always ask.

Simulations

Almost at the other end of the spectrum of training methods from activity courses, simulations focus attention very specifically on one area of activity. Their teaching is then through involvement, often with technology lending a hand. Typically a computer program provides the basis to experiment with complex interactions.

For example there are simulations used in marketing training. They set up a market situation: products, prices, people, markets, competitors and more. Decision-making can be input and not only recorded, but also recorded in such a way that the whole complex web of "given" factors changes. Thus a decision to raise a product's price will see volume sold and profitability adjusted accordingly while competition taking action in response can also be seen. Some such training devices are for individuals to use, others work – sometimes competitively – with a group of people participating together.

They can provide considerable realism and considerable stimulation. They tend not to be suitable as a first exposure to a topic, relying as they do on the participants having some knowledge of the subject.

They need clear briefing and sometimes preparatory work to set them up, but this is understandable given their role and purpose.

If you want to check out this sort of thing, a good example is a marketing training device called Markstrat. The organization producing this, and it is one that has been around a while and is therefore tried and tested, is StratX Ltd. If you check their Website it will give you a flavor of how it all works: (www.stratx.com).

Packaged training

This term is usually used to describe training resources with two characteristics. First, they use a variety of aids to package their training: such include audio and video material, programmed learning texts, and, of course, computer based training particularly using CD-ROMs. Secondly, they are designed to work on a, sometimes largely unsupervised, solo basis or, if with a group, through "facilitation" (someone to lead the way through, rather than act as a fully fledged trainer).

The simplest form will set participants off down a road. They work through a workbook. They pause on occasion as they do so: to view video clips, listen to audio elements, answer questions (which with programmed learning devices can redirect them, recapping if knowledge is not proven to be at a certain level) or, where group work is involved, to interact with others.

If you can find good things in this sort of format, and you may find them in libraries or be able to persuade your company to finance them (pointing out that they are then a permanent asset and that once you have used them other people can do so too. Much that is packaged is also now computerized, for more details see Chapter 4.

Open learning

This phrase is used to encapsulate a number of techniques linking work done "at your desk" to a central point elsewhere that coordinates the activity (hence the alternative description of distance learning). This has become a popular way of handling the load of studying for some sort of qualification – where exercises, projects and such like are set and marked by tutors at the body offering the course. Study may involve all sorts of mixtures of method, from reading to watching videos, and, of course, computer work (some now on-line).

The principle is also used for job-based training and an open learning setup may exist in a large organization where staff work in many widely spread locations.

Resource centers

These are often the preserve of larger companies. The idea developed from the simple library and that element remains. Beyond that, however, the resource center has a range of developmental materials and the equipment they demand. Here someone can go and watch a video, spend time at a dedicated computer learning station, engage in certain small group activities – or just find a helpful book or a word of advice.

There is no one definition of a resource center. Different organizations configure them differently, and of course they change over time. Not only do they provide an aid to learning, their very existence contributes to the creation of a development culture, demonstrates that development is important and helps both managers and staff fit undertaking it into a busy life.

Job rotation and swapping

There are a variety of ways to incorporate development into the everyday work of the organization. Sometimes this is simply a matter of change. People are intentionally moved into new jobs, rather different to what they were doing previously, for developmental reason. There is a "domino effect" as people move round and thus many other people are affected by the moves. I deal with some organizations where this is an established pattern: no one expects to stay in the same post for more than a short number of years. Not only is this seen as aiding the development of the individuals concerned, it is regarded as stimulating the new thinking and new ideas necessary to prevent the organization becoming stuck in a rut. It also may benefit staff retention (people are less likely to leave through boredom). This may or may not be something your employer does as a routine, but there is no reason why you cannot make suggestions even about a one-off idea.

Films

Training films cover the topic of sales well and all the major providers have titles addressing sales and allied issues. They do not offer complete training in a moment, but they do offer good encapsulations of principles and illustrate matters in a memorable way (or the good ones do). They are quite expensive to buy or even to hire, but you can make suggestions about using them at sales meetings, look at them in a resource center if you have one or attend the previews that seem regularly scheduled for assessment purposes.

Secondment

For some companies a good, and convenient, way of developing people is to post them for longer or shorter periods away from their present location. This may simply be to a branch office (or from a branch to HQ). Or to a location where activity is specialized: a research facility perhaps.

For multinationals and others involved in business internationally, the tactic may typically involve overseas postings (or indeed job rotation). I was witness to this just recently when a relative of mine moved to the corporate headquarters of his (American) employer – Procter & Gamble – in the USA. This costs more than recruiting locally (he has four children to swell the costs!), but has a broader intention than just filling a post. Careers are not preordained of course, but the thinking here is that all being well he will return (or go elsewhere in the organization) having acquired experience to jump him up the corporate hierarchy faster than continuing to work in his home base would have done.

Some policy and guidelines for those seeking such opportunities may exist in a large organization (I doubt if it is a novel occurrence in Procter & Gamble). In other circumstances it is again something to consider and suggest, though it may need a persuasive case to be made.

There are various opportunities here, not all limited to large multinationals. For example, secondment may be arranged:

» in a different division of an organization;
» in a subsidiary company;
» with a customer (or supplier) organization;

» with the organization of an agent or distributor; or
» with a professional body (some of which are supported by their member companies seconding staff to them for a while; usually where there is reciprocal benefit).

It could be round the corner, up three flights of stairs or thousands of miles away. You may well be able to think of, or use, other forms of secondment. Swaps - exchanges - are possible also, organized so that two people, and both organizational parties, benefit. This kind of arrangement might be essentially short term, say a week in the Paris office. Or, more relevant in this chapter, it might mean swapping roles and locations for a year or more.

Sabbaticals

Here is something that will perhaps be regarded as something of a luxury. But it can have real value, and be cost effective too. It can take various forms, but in one company I worked with, one category of senior people were allowed to take six months (paid) leave after working with the company for fifteen years. In consultancy - a fee earning and time dependent business - this represented a significant cost. Equally it was a business in which many did not habitually take long holidays because of the nature of the business, so in some ways the time was, in part, a quid pro quo.

Certainly it was highly motivational, both to those in the prescribed category and to those who aspired to be. I cannot now remember whether it was compulsory to do so, but such extended periods of leave often included a project, something to which no time would otherwise be given. For example, travel was one thing people sometimes wanted to do, and this linked usefully to the international development of the business allowing more leisurely research and investigation than might otherwise have occurred. If this were coupled with some fee earning work it made good sense all round.

There are a number of variables here, certainly the:

» duration selected;
» number and level of staff to be involved;
» purpose (or lack of it) given to the gap period; and
» reporting back, if appropriate.

One can think of all sorts of things this system could be used for, and one is certainly development. This is something else to seek out or suggest, perhaps.

NO STONE UNTURNED

A complete list of methods is neither possible here nor is it intended. Indeed the inventive sales person will keep any list they do have expanding as time goes by.

It is worth putting yourself in a position to check, quickly and regularly what is possible, what is new and what else you can do. Thus is may be worthwhile to:

» subscribe to various trade, business or specifically sales journals;
» subscribe to relevant newsletters and e-zines delivered automatically to your computer;
» allow your name to be added certain mailing lists (for instance to get news of the latest products produced by a training film company whose preview meetings you might attend);
» occasionally (regularly?) attend relevant exhibitions (for example a trade show to improve competitor intelligence or a training exhibition to see what new development aids might be available and useful); and
» cultivate a friend in the HR department (or similar) especially if you are in a large organization, or indeed anyone else who gives access to useful information.

Self development is an open-ended process. Some things can be adopted on a regular basis, undertaking them can become a positive habit. Other things are more occasional, or one-off, and everything must be assessed regularly to see if it is still useful or if your mix of development activity should contain something else instead. The next section looks at further details about methods, and illustrates more about how things work and what works best.

Self Development in Practice

This chapter considers the current practice and examines how self development methods can work for you. In particular it looks at:

» obtaining and using feedback;
» getting the most from management; and
» getting the most from training courses.

"You grab a challenge, act on it, then honestly reflect on why your actions worked or didn't. You learn from it and then move on. That continuing process of lifelong learning helps enormously in a rapidly changing economic environment."

John Kotter, Harvard Business School

A plethora of development methods was touched on in Chapter 6, and the point made that everything needs to be considered in light of clear intentions and objectives. With that still in mind we look in this section at how some of these methods can work for you. The methods and examples selected are chosen, not to be comprehensive, rather to illustrate the mix of activities that can be used, either taken advantage of or prompted, and the manageability and effectiveness of such a mix.

OBTAINING AND USING FEEDBACK

The first thing to concentrate on that allows regular and useful self development is feedback. Where does this come from? Essentially there are three sources:

1 *Your manager:* feedback will in all probability be offered from your manager and a formal and ongoing system of working practice needs to be developed between the two of you (see next main heading). Beyond that remember that it is as much for you to suggest things as wait for them to be offered and that the simple principle of asking questions can provide a great deal of information.
2 *Your colleagues:* this category includes your peers in the sales team, or similar people with whom you can share experience if you are not a full-time sales person. It also includes others around your organization; some, like the training manager, have already been mentioned.
3 *Your customers:* your experience with these should provide you with endless feedback just through observation. Ask yourself: what did I say and do, how did I do it and what was the reaction? Note honestly the facts and resolve to learn from them. But you can do more than this; you can ask. Carefully, select customers most likely to be prepared to welcome this kind of exchange, and without implying that you are the best sales person ever. The thing to test here is not

technique – what did you think of my close? – but reactions. Ask whether your frequency of call suits them, ask if you seem to get through things in a suitable amount of time, ask if the level of detail you go into is sufficient, ask if they need more evidence. The answers to these kinds of question are always useful. Sometimes answers can be surprising. For example, I have regularly talked to sales people who have had to adapt their approach to take up less time with customers, though it only became clear when they were asked. Previously they had been polite enough to say nothing.

In obtaining and using feedback you are essentially looking for two things.

» *Signs of weakness:* what do you do that could be done better? It pays to adopt a positive and constructive attitude to criticism. It is very easy to allow an instinctive defensive reaction to blind you to lessons that can be useful. In any case, most often you are not going to be told you are total rubbish, and may only need to make minor adjustments to ensure that something is significantly improved.
» *Strengths:* it is just as important to discover what goes well. This is not simply so that you can pat yourself on the back (though a little self-motivation does no harm), it is again so that you can fine-tune your approach. Ask yourself how you can build on strengths, where you can use something more or in different ways. Again this kind of process is a sure path to improved performance.

To make any activity of this sort work you need a clear idea of the areas on which you should focus. At one level it is easy.

» How did you start the sales meeting?
» How quickly did you establish a rapport?
» How clearly and thoroughly did you identify needs?
» Was the case you made clear, attractive and credible?
» How well did you deal with any objections that came up?
» Did you close and close effectively?

But such a list only highlights the classic stages of a sales interview. You may want to focus on more, including:

» how well you prepared;
» your time management;
» territory management and organization;
» customer records;
» product knowledge;
» imaginative description;
» use of sales aids;
» addition of evidence of what you say;
» the tailoring of your approach to an individual customer;
» management and direction of the overall interview;
» parting impression;
» follow-up action;
» display of empathy;
» persistence;
» professionalism (asking what characteristics you must display to be thought so); and
» productivity.

You can doubtless extend and personalize this sort of list. For example, you may want to monitor the description you give of a specific product within the range, or try to encapsulate what you have to say within a specific amount of time.

Much of what needs to be done here is made easier by habit. Some sales people seem to emerge from every meeting they conduct with something to carry forward and which they can use to assist the next one; it makes sense. So does getting others to help you.

GETTING THE MOST FROM MANAGEMENT

Three particular ways of interacting with your manager are focused on here.

1 *Ongoing counseling (usually involving accompanied calling, evaluation and a link to development of all sorts):* most managers will evaluate what any sales person is doing and what results they are getting. While a bad manager may see this as just looking at the figures and shouting when targets are missed, many see this role more

constructively. They take the view that even the best performance can be improved and act to do just that. The most practical way in which this happens is through joint calling. The manager will link attending some calls with you, ideally on a regular basis, with a counseling session to review strengths and weaknesses (what is sometimes called "the roadside conference" as it sometimes takes place in the car after a call). This can seem intrusive, but remember it is the *only* way in which they can observe and investigate how you do things (sitting at their desk they can only see the figures: what comes from what you do). So this is something to be approached constructively. Take on board what they say, ask questions, try things out on them and use them as a sounding board. Selling can be a lonely business – make use of time spent to analyze and help take your approaches and skills forward. This is a sales specific form of what is more generally called "training-on-the-job".

2 *Sales meetings:* every so often the sales team will get together; this may be weekly, monthly – whatever, the frequency depends on such factors as cost and geography. No matter how often this happens you want to get the most from it. Again a good manager will see this as an opportunity to inform, motivate, gather and exchange ideas – and undertake development activities. It is sometimes a problem to keep such meetings fresh, indeed they can settle into a repetitive format and a bit of a rut. So do not be backward in making suggestions or volunteering to initiate action in this area (you might collaborate with colleagues in so doing – "a number of us think . . ."). A number of things are possible.

» *Training games and exercises:* these are designed to focus attention on one particular aspect of the job (this might include something as simple as a quiz to check product knowledge through to elaborate, often team, exercises).

» *Role playing:* this is a classic way of experimenting with an interactive skill like selling. Simple versions of it can be used in just a few minutes in a sales meeting (see box p. 60).

» *Brainstorming:* as a route to generating ideas this can work well (though it needs to be properly set up and carried out – see example p. 62).

EXAMPLE: ROLE-PLAYING

Formal role-play can be an inherent part of a training session or course. It may involve using audio or video equipment to record the role-play so that replaying it can form the basis of more detailed critique designed to lead to change. Equally, it can be used much less formally at a sales meeting: for example, using carousel role-play (where two people start a conversation – in this case between buyer and seller – and then two others take over and run the conversation on; it can thus involve a whole group very quickly).

Although role-play is a tried and tested technique and there is no reason for it not to work well, it does need some care. Certainly there are things that can jeopardize its success. Be careful of potential dangers including:

» over-awareness of the camera;
» overacting to the camera, indeed a belief that role play demands "acting";
» the difficulty of being "on show" in front of peers;
» poor role-play briefs (ask if you are not sure what you are trying to do);
» incomplete or unconstructive feedback after the role play is complete (again ask); and
» those watching feeling excluded (ask for or suggest an observer role).

More positively, role-play can be organized to avoid the above and can achieve one or more of the following.

» Reproduce real life as closely as possible.
» Allow practice of important, difficult or unusual situations.
» Introduce and practice a skill new to people.
» Develop confidence.
» Experiment with new approaches.
» Change negative habits or reinforce positive ones.

» Reinforce knowledge and instill useful reflexes.
» Utilize analytical skills (used in the feedback and critique).

All these are things you should recognize as being worthwhile. Role-play offers a safe environment. It may be a touch awkward to role-play in front of colleagues, but it is much better to practice and experiment with new ideas in this way before risking all on a real customer.

EXAMPLE: BRAINSTORMING – GUIDELINES FOR SUCCESS

Brainstorming is a group activity and can be used to provide an almost instant burst of idea generation. Working with a group of people (maybe three or four up to a dozen works most easily) it needs a prescribed approach, as in the following.

» Gather people around and explain the objectives (what exactly are ideas required about and why).
» Explain that there are to be *no comments* on ideas at this stage.
» Allow a little time for thought (singly or, say, in pairs).
» Start taking contributions and noting them down (publicly on say a flipchart).
» When a good-sized list is established and recorded, then analysis can begin.
» Grouping similar ideas together can make the list more manageable.
» Open-minded discussion can then review the list.
» Identify ideas that can be taken forward.

Such a session must exclude the word "impossible" from the conversation, at least initially (and especially when used in senses such as "It's impossible, we don't do things that way" (why not?), or "It's impossible, we tried it once and it didn't work"(how long ago and in what form?).

By avoiding any negative or censorious first responses, by allowing one idea to spark another and variations on a theme to refine a point (perhaps taking it from something wild to something practical), a brainstorming session can produce genuinely new approaches.

It can be fun to do, satisfying in outcome and time-efficient to undertake – and a group which brainstorms regularly gets better at it, and quicker and more certain in their production of good, useable, ideas. It is something to suggest perhaps, as well as to participate in, however it occurs.

3 *Job performance appraisal* (the classic "annual" appraisal): The point has been made about taking a constructive approach to various systems and processes within the organization. None has such wide-ranging influence as the (often annual) job appraisal. You have to resolve and act to get the most from it. A useful (rather than a "good") appraisal:

» focuses your thinking, and your subsequent development plan, on areas that need attention – that is both strengths and weaknesses;

» provides immediate feedback and counseling which can be useful;

» gives you the opportunity to make suggestions regarding company sponsored development activity; and

» sets up actual development activities that can form the core of your own, perhaps, more extensive, plan.

These points focus on the development side of appraisal. It is also an opportunity to project the right image, consider long-term career development and, not least, to link to the specific job to be done over the coming year. A good manager will always take a constructive view of appraisal; realistically it is something that some companies organize less than perfectly and which some managers find awkward to do. It certainly warrants your taking a suitable initiative to help ensure it is as useful for you as possible.

Remember too that an appraisal meeting is not a one-off event, it may well – indeed should – link to other conversations of various sorts throughout the year, and you need to get the most from these too. The checklist below acts to sum up the key issues.

EXAMPLE: TAKING A CONSTRUCTIVE APPROACH TO YOUR APPRAISAL

Specifically, you need to set yourself objectives under a number of headings.

» Planning how to make positive points about performance during the period under review.
» Being ready to respond to points raised, including negative ones, appropriately.
» Projecting the right image.
» Reviewing specific work plans for the next period ahead.
» Reviewing factors on which success in the future depends.
» Identifying the need or desirability for training and development.
» Looking ahead to longer term career development.
» Linking discussion to salary and benefits review.

The key to getting the most from appraisals can be summarized in ten key points, as follows.

1 Take appraisal seriously (it is a luxury to be able to step back and think about what you are doing).
2 View it constructively – focus on what you (and your organization) can gain from it.
3 Study and become familiar with the system your organization uses.
4 Keep appraisals in mind during the year and gather the facts and information that will help your next one.
5 Prepare thoroughly for the meeting, thinking of what you want to discuss and anticipating what will be raised.
6 Aim to play an active part in the meeting, rather than simply be led by events.

7 Put your points over clearly and positively.

8 Ask anything where you feel comment or information would be helpful.

9 Record and action points agreed during the meeting (and be sure to hit any deadlines for action agreed).

10 Be open in discussion, constructive about criticism, positive about opportunities for the future and always receptive to new ways of doing things and new things you might do.

Though all appraisals may have to address strengths and weaknesses of performance, one that is simply unconstructive and from which nothing useful flows is just a waste of time. Company systems may demand that appraisals are gone through, perhaps for reasons of employment legislation, but if they are going to be done then the best should be got from them. Of course this is dependent on both you and the management; but make sure you play your part in making it constructive.

Note: the above checklist is adapted from the book *Career Skills* also in the ExpressExec series.

All in all, your manager is the best resource you are likely to have available to assist your development. Not only should they help in the way that they work with you, but they should also make possible other things that are then implemented on your own – for instance in the training they allow or instigate.

GETTING THE MOST FROM TRAINING COURSES

Some companies issue guidelines for those attending formal courses, whether external or internal. These may be useful and worth studying for a moment. As an example, the boxed paragraph that follows is one set of guidelines given to people attending public courses. Originally devised by American consultant Bob Whitney, and set out in the book *Running an Effective Training Session* (Gower Publishing), it certainly addresses some of the key issues and sets the scene for getting the most from the experience of attending.

NOTES FOR DELEGATES: AN EXAMPLE OF A DOCUMENT ISSUED TO DELEGATES AT THE START OF A COURSE (OR AHEAD OF ATTENDANCE)

1 This manual contains all the basic details of this training program. Further papers will be distributed progressively during the course so that a complete record will be available by the last session.

2 This is *your* seminar, and represents a chance to say what you think – so please do say it. Everyone can learn from the comments of others and the discussion it prompts.

3 Exchange of experience is as valuable as the formal lectures – but you need to *listen carefully* and try to understand other points of view if this is to work.

4 Do support your views with facts in discussion, use examples and stick to the point.

5 Keep questions and comments succinct – do not monopolize the proceedings, but let others have a say so that various viewpoints can be discussed.

6 Make points in context as they arise. Remember that participation is an attitude of mind. It includes listening as well as speaking, but also certainly includes constructive disagreement where appropriate.

7 Make notes as the meeting progresses. There is notepaper provided in this binder. Formal notes will provide an aide memoir of the content and coverage, so any additional notes should primarily link to your job and to action on your return to work. Even a few action points noted per session can act as a catalyst and help ensure action follows attendance.

8 A meeting with colleagues, staff or your manager on your return to normal working can be valuable, it acts as a bridge

between ideas discussed here and action in the workplace and can make change more likely.

9 It will help everyone present if you wear your name badge, respect the timetable and keep mobile telephones and pagers switched off during the sessions.

10 This is an opportunity to step back from day to day operations and consider issues that can help make your job more effective. Be skeptical of your own operation, challenge ideas, remain open minded throughout and actively seek new thinking that can help you prompt change and improve performance.

Whether your organization produces something like this or not, these are sensible points and it is certainly always worth having such principles in mind when you attend any kind of formal session.

MAKING IT HAPPEN, MAKING IT WORK

A host of developmental things can be done and made to work if you think constructively and broadly about fitting them to the day-to-day work as the following examples show.

» In one financial services organization, sales jobs routinely involved making formal "on-your-feet" presentations. In addition to undergoing training, people needed practice. At the suggestion of one team member certain internal meetings adopted a rule that anyone making a significant contribution had to stand up to do so. Effectively this increased the number of presentations people made, and provided an opportunity for comment and critique which assisted the way skills were developed.

» In a publishing company one sales person told me that she made a point of observing certain competitive sales people (with much selling taking place in open areas of bookshops, a little judicious browsing made this easy to do). "Both what they do, and how buyers react, lead to good ideas and allows me to make positive adjustments to my approach", she said. Good idea and a number of industries work in a way that allows this to be done.

MATCH TO THE SALES JOB

Productivity is important, but so too is relaxation; all work and no play makes Jack a dull boy as the saying has it. So at this stage it should be recognized that the overall intention here is to put together an appropriate and manageable mix of development activity, not to unreasonably utilize every waking moment. That said, you should at least consider the way you work and see what possibilities this suggests. Two examples, one major, one minor, may help to make the point.

» *Car audio:* how far do you drive each year? More apposite still given today's traffic conditions, how long do you spend in the car? Some of that time could be spent doing something useful (and safer than talking on a mobile phone). Virtually all cars have a tape or CD player in them and a wealth of useful material is available in this form, specifically:
  » some companies issue newsletters or product briefings or training in this form;
  » a variety of business books, are available on tape;
  » sales training material is available in this form too, including audio seminar material, cases and (mostly American) inspirational material; and
  » time spent listening to such material can be useful, interesting and stress busting (making you forget that traffic jam about which you can do nothing) – it can provide a constructive moment or a long-term project (for example, you could learn a language).
» *Screensaver:* another opportunity to turn idle moments to use or to remind yourself of something key needed in your selling; for the computer literate, certainly for the computer enthusiast, you can install information in this way.

DEVELOPMENT CIRCLES

Some years ago the Japanese were using a technique, taken up around the world in various ways, called quality circles. The idea was that a continuous focus could be kept on quality (primarily in a factory and production context) and a flow of ideas generated, the best of which could be taken up, implemented and used to increase productivity.

Circles, groups of people of a size to facilitate discussion, were set up. Over time they looked at a whole series of issues (e.g. something with a specific description such as reducing waste of raw materials in a particular phase of production) and essentially brainstormed the matter. Ideas were fed up the organization, through a hierarchy of groups, the best and most practical being approved by management and coordinated into operations. Communication was organized to be two-way so that everyone knew what was being achieved.

The basic principle of a permanent, or semi-permanent, organization of people focused on improvements has been copied and modified and made to work usefully in many different contexts since the idea of quality circles originated. Another area on which a similar approach has been used is that of customer service.

This sort of procedure can, like brainstorming on its own, produce learning in the area of creativity. Arranged with this sort of formality it can also direct people towards a whole range of other useful skills. Someone has to chair the sessions, people have to listen and contribute. Matters have to be reported back up the line, reports written and presentations made. An element of competition and incentive has often been used to add to people's concentration (a bonus payment for the team producing the most valuable idea, perhaps).

Thus such a scheme can be used overtly or otherwise to progress a variety of development aims with some of these skills in mind. This is a good example of development and operational activity being progressed usefully alongside each other so that both gain.

> "Knowledge is of two kinds. We know a subject ourselves, or we know where we can find information upon it."
>
> *Samuel Johnson*

An old and wise saying, and much about self development relates to it. You ask too many questions, of yourself and of others. Cultivating a compulsive asking disorder makes good sense for the intelligent self developer.

Key Resources and Thinkers

This chapter consists of:

- » a glossary for self development for sales people;
- » key concepts in the field; and
- » key thinkers in the field.

"There will be more confusion in the business world in the next decade than in any decade in history. And the current pace of change will only accelerate."

Steve Case, Chairman, AOL Time Warner

Explaining the details of the techniques of selling is not part of our brief here (but see the ExpressExec volumes *Selling* and *Selling a Service*), so the terminology that follows is primarily concerned with development.

GLOSSARY

The intention here is not to list terms defining the sales job itself in detail (though other volumes in the series do this), rather it is to reflect the focus on the self development inherent in this title.

Appraisal (or job, performance or staff appraisal) – the formal process of evaluation, manifest primarily in the regular – often annual – appraisal interview, that links performance in one period with goals and targets for the next.

Brainstorming – a technique for originating new ideas through group interaction.

Career commitment – term used to describe the psychological state of being committed to working actively to enhance your career prospects.

Career ladder – a formal path laid down by an organization as a guide to how an employee would likely progress; now much less in evidence and much less likely to be a guaranteed guide.

Career management – the process in context of which our topic here is reviewed: it is the personal systematic, ongoing planning and fine-tuning of objectives and action that is designed to progress a career.

Career planning – most usually applied to the corporate intention to guide people along a particular path (remember that such a path does not necessarily match an individual's requirements accurately), though it can equally be applied to what an individual should do.

Career plan – the plan that states personal goals and intentions as the basis for career management.

Computer learning – an umbrella term for the plethora of developmental and training activities that can, in some way, be delivered utilizing a computer as all or part of their methodology.

Course – this is a generic term for a training event. They come in all shapes and sizes and the terminology used for the many types (workshop, seminar, conference etc.) is curiously vague. The key elements that characterize different kind of event are the number of participants and the nature and amount of participation involved.

Curriculum vitae (résumé) – this is the written statement of a career to date used in attempting to move on (internally or externally); it needs keeping up to date and importantly it should describe not just the facts of employment, but the achievements of work done and significant development has a place here.

Development gap – the gap between the competences that exist and those necessary to do the job now or in the future upon which development objectives are focused.

Development circle – scheme akin to the Japanese idea of quality circles, here extended to focus on areas other than quality (including increasing sales) and which link learning, idea generation and action.

E-learning – the current word for what used to be described as computer learning. It incorporates elements delivered via the Internet or intranet and thus extends the meaning of the earlier term.

Exit interviews – interviews held as people leave work aimed at discovering why they leave in order to assist improve recruitment policy and practice. Though not designed primarily to help people in their careers they can be useful. Sometimes the same sort of thing is done when people move internally (to a new division or location, perhaps) and that may be something else from which the careerist can learn.

Fast track – sometimes used as a formal term for employees selected to be moved through a career path, usually early in their career, on an accelerated basis; also a general term for rapid progress. An enhanced amount of development is often inherent in such an arrangement.

Job enlargement – this is an expansion of work activities and responsibilities. It can be positive or may sometimes be a way for the organization to get more output without paying for it. Certainly it is usually something that can accelerate learning and experience.

Job redesign – as with "sideways move," this is usually a negative term implying action to keep someone at the same level. Watch out, this may teach you nothing.

Job rotation – the specific strategy used by some organizations which moves people from one job to another as a general philosophy of ringing the changes, rather than because of the merits of an individual move. It is felt to create positive motivation by enhancing job satisfaction and to stimulate creativity and retention; again it can enhance learning and accelerate experience.

Job satisfaction – all the elements of interest, satisfaction, fun, challenge and more that can come from working; one aim of self development is surely to increase this.

Job sharing – the way of working that covers one job with two (or more people) working on a part time basis. Although not the prime reason for the arrangement, it can provide a collaborator for mutual development.

Kerbside (or roadside) conference – see on-the-job training.

Lifelong learning – the generic term for the overall principle of learning continuing throughout life, a process made necessary by the greater change inherent in any career path in a dynamic work environment.

Learning lifeline – this term, coined by Eddy Knasel, John Meed and Anna Rosetti, the authors of *Learn for your Life*, suggests a concept of continuity, with analysis of past learning and objectives linking to and assisting future plans.

Mentoring – this constitutes counseling given to someone by someone other than their line manager, usually on a regular basis at least for a period.

Networking – the skill of keeping in touch with people or managing contacts. There really is an art to doing this in a way that is truly useful and yet does not become unduly time-consuming or an end in itself. Stands investigation as an essential career management and development tool.

On-the-job training – means ongoing informal training or development activity that occurs through interaction between someone and their boss as the actual job is carried out. In sales the core interaction itself is sometimes called the "road or kerbside conference" (because it may take place in a car after a call on a customer).

Portfolio career – this is a term for working in a way that allows you to do more than one thing. It is predominantly used in context of those who are self-employed or in small businesses (for example, the author of this work operates in writing, training and consultancy), but is increasingly possible in larger organizations as well; it may be a useful first step to a career change. The wider the scope of what you do, or will do in the future, the greater the number of areas that development must address.

Sales meeting – a regular gathering of the members of a field sales team; normally ongoing development is one of its remits.

Resource center – a dedicated and specialized "library" within an organization that is designed as an adjunct to formal training and development. Usually a library-like environment its facilities range from books to those enabling e-learning or the viewing of training films. Though much of its purpose is job related, it provides a means for the individual to link development and career advancement. Check it out if you have one in your company.

Rewards (and remuneration) – this is simply payment for employment. The key thing here is to remember that both are umbrella terms and that a plethora of benefits may be involved alongside salary. There is a relationship between development, the increasing competence it creates, a broadening role or improved results, and the payment made for what someone does which it pays (*sic*) to keep an eye on.

Role-playing – this involves practice of an interactive skill (like selling) through "play acting" a scenario. For example creating a conversation between two people, one playing the buyer and one the seller. It is a classic training technique and ideal for experimenting with new approaches.

Sabbatical – an absence from work, sometimes for a period of weeks or months, taken in part as relaxation and change which often has a development intention within it focusing on something that could only be done given real time away from the job (it is an exceptional circumstance, sometimes earned by long service).

Sideways move – literally a move of job that changes work and responsibilities but does not move a person up the hierarchy; sometimes euphemistically called "sideways promotion".

Succession planning – succession refers to those who follow people into key positions should they leave, and the concept of operating on the basis that internal promotion is always an option wherever possible. Given the importance of this it is perhaps curious that in some organizations it is taken very seriously, while in others it is ignored. If you hanker after your boss' job, it may well be worth knowing what plans, if any, exist should they leave. Your self-development might therefore then be directed at a very specific end.

KEY CONCEPTS

In learning

Those in selling with a strong careerist outlook will embrace the concept of self development, working to maximize the usefulness of development offered and taking action to add to this in order to fulfill their own intentions. It follows that it is useful to keep an eye on processes and developments in the world of training and development so as to be able to utilize anything that may help. The following factors are examples. They range wide from overall approaches to learning to specific and focused techniques.

Open learning – a course of learning that the learner takes at their own pace, working independently yet tapping into a central point to receive various tutorial or group inputs. This term embraces many forms, and these days overlaps with e-learning (see below).

E-learning – this is most recently defined as learning delivered over the Internet or intranet, though it is also used more generally to describe anything with a high technology component to its delivery and overlaps with a wealth of other terminology such as computer learning. This has a section of its own earlier in this text – see Chapter 4.

Resource center – we are all familiar with a library. A resource center is a library that combines the material and the means to take it in across a wide variety of formats and methodology. For instance, you might find a useful training film in a resource center and be able to view it there and then on equipment provided within the center. Many individual companies have such facilities, so to do other bodies such as colleges or trade bodies.

Programmed learning – this crosses over somewhat with open learning. Most often this is a short module, something which can be worked through and which introduces checks as you go to ensure learning on one point before moving onto the next. The method of delivery can vary: manual, computer and more.

Action learning – at its simplest this is training and development that includes participation in a form that provides practice and thus links learning and utilization of new skills more promptly and directly.

Emotional intelligence – David Goleman coined this term. Essentially a prescribed approach to communication and interpersonal relationships it defines an approach in which a person is: self-aware, understands and manages their emotions, is actively self-motivating, has good empathy and manages the overall process of creating and maintaining a relationship. Customer/supplier relationships are just the sort of thing this approach addresses.

Neurolinguistic programming – NLP, as it has become known, is again at the behavioral end of the scale. It links the therapy skills of using the way we experience the world around us and the experiences it gives us, with the language we use to order our own thoughts and behavior and communicate with others. This too has applications in sales communication.

Role-playing – because interactive skills are difficult to learn by note as it were, role-playing has long been used in sales training (and other areas of interactive communications skills). The idea of two, or more people, acting out a scenario playing parts on the sales and buying side of an interaction and using it to explore and practice skills is well proven and very useful. It provides something close to real life, and therefore closely linked to the job, and yet safe – there being no real customer from whom to lose a deal. First experience of role-play can be awkward, or even embarrassing. It is, however, not something to resist. Formally or informally, and it is used in various ways, when well planned it is constructive and useful. If the opportunity occurs, give it a go and treat it constructively. You may learn a great deal from it.

You may wisely keep an eye on such techniques and on developments in these kinds of area, investigating or making use of those that seem best suited to your intentions and goals.

In selling

It is similarly sensible to maintain a wide appreciation of sales processes and techniques. It is beyond the brief of this volume to review the whole sales process and how it works (though other titles do just that). Here suffice to say that you can do worse than organize your thinking in this area so that you have a clear idea of what you want to keep up with. Categories might include the following.

» Sales concepts and techniques.
» Broader business concepts and techniques, perhaps especially over-lapping into the world of marketing.
» Industry concepts and ideas: your and those of your customers.
» Technological factors as they affect the area in which you work.
» Economic and political concepts and policies (for example, if you sell say radar equipment you may want to be able to appear knowledgeable about factors affecting their sale overseas for military use).

Whatever your field of work may encompass, it is worth taking a broad view of the range of things with which you might need to involve yourself or of which you need some understanding.

In career management

It is worth remembering that self-development is part of the larger activity of career management. Here activity needs to be actively directed at a plethora of tasks from surviving in the complex, and often less than benign, environment of the modern workplace and organization to enhancing your career prospects and taking action designed to move you on and up.

This is too big a topic to do more than touch on here. I have recently written on it at more length in the Wiley *Kickstart* series book *Corporate Survival.*

KEY THINKERS

Again, we take learning and content separately. This time consider content first. There are few key thinkers in the sense of people who have cast unique insights into the selling process. The nearest to this is an organization rather than an individual.

Huthwaite Research Group

Without doubt one organization has added a whole new dimension to the way sales and selling are viewed, and thus to the practice of sale management; that is Huthwaite Research Group Ltd. It is better known for its trademark SPIN and the approach to selling this applies. Starting in the early 70s they applied new techniques to the observation of selling. Using behavior analysis, a research technique for observing and quantifying interactions between buyer and seller, it highlighted the interactive skills that seemed to best create successful sales. Key amongst them was questioning.

The main focus of their studies was on:

» how people buy and weigh up competitive offerings to help them make considered decisions;
» reactions, particularly negative ones, that buyers tend to have to being sold to;
» qualities that buyers regard as making a case (verbally or in writing) attractive, persuasive and credible; and
» the style of selling approach that appeared to be best regarded.

The fact that their views were based on and validated by research – literally thousands of interviews and observations of real sales meetings – was novel, they might say unique. In any case it was a key factor in helping make sales a profession. They offered training with sales techniques recommended by and matched to their studies, and their base of sales training has expanded to a full range of topics, including sales, negotiation, account management, major account strategies and sales management.

Though many would suggest that the Huthwaite research highlighted, at least in part, approaches that were either common sense, or which had been documented earlier by others, their success in promoting their ideas certainly gave prominence to a very practical and logical way of looking at selling.

The key to the approach is customer focus. Once selling was regarded as something "you did to people," now it is predominantly seen as a process of helping and working with the psychological process by which people make decisions to buy. Key therefore is the concept of discovering, through very specifically applied questioning techniques (this is where the patented SPIN technique comes in), exactly what is going on at the customer's side of the discussion. If sales people find out about a customer, how they think, what they need, how they operate and what their expectations are of their suppliers and those that represent them, they will more precisely be able to focus their sales approach. The concept of the sales professional and of the sales person as advisor is also key to the approach. This may seem less than novel now, but everything about selling that builds in these kinds of approaches (wherever they come from) tends to work best in the real world.

The need for an intelligent approach to selling, and an avoidance of any hint of "selling by rote" makes this an area well worth exploring. Neil Rackham of Huthwaite Research has also written extensively. His books include the following.

» *Making Major Sales*
» *Account Strategy for Major Sales*
» *The Management of Major Sales* (written with Richard Ruff)
» *Getting Partnering Right*

One or more of these may be worth a look.

Behavioral approaches to selling

The techniques of selling should reflect the fact that it is an interactive communications skill. As has been said, it is not so much intellectually taxing as something that demands careful appreciation and then orchestration of its various elements. That said a number of approaches are documented that stress the behavioral aspects of selling, particularly of complex sales and sales of intangibles. Two worth noting are:

» *Kepner/Tregoe:* the founders of this consultancy and training company were Charles H. *Kepner* and Benjamin B. *Tregoe*. Their book *The New Rational Manager* is a well-known text, and the relevance to selling is in the link between their view that managers (and thus buyers) like to make decisions through a systematic approach and thus that selling and account planning needs to match this approach.

» *Mark Hanan:* his book, *Consultative Selling,* is perhaps the best example reviewing the need to base selling in so many situations on "becoming your customer's partner." The logic is clear: customers making decisions to deal with a supplier put themselves in their hands, in extreme cases their business may literally stand or fall through the actions of a key supplier (say of components). Certainly they see a suitable supplier as an adjunct to their creating the profitability that they seek. Again a detailed understanding of the feelings and motivation of customers helps the sales process.

Other people have reviewed the sales area in a variety of ways (and books of various sorts are commented on further in the next section).

As sales people will wisely address self development with a wide brief, it is also worth checking other leading writers in two categories.

» *Marketing:* as selling is a component part of the marketing mix, and a possible career avenue for progress too, it may be worthwhile to investigate key writers here. This might include the ultimate guru of marketing, Philip Kotler, particularly his briefer books (such as *Kotler on Marketing*). It might range wider depending on your interests.

» *The broader business world:* what you need to do here depends on your job, your ambitions and the industry or technical area in which you work.

The sales role puts you at the sharp end of things. Those who do best will take a broad view and also will match their background reading and research to make it fit the area in which they – and their customers – work.

Resources

This chapter is examines key resources in professional organizations, books, magazines, research and qualifications.

"Information is not the pathway to enlightenment, happiness or wisdom. Information is only data, after all, and it is possible to have too much of it. In fact, information can get in the way of wisdom unless we leave ourselves sufficient time and energy to reflect on it, make sense of it, and integrate it into our lives."

Hugh Mackay, Australian market researcher and writer

To get what you need to do in context of the "learning organization: read *The Fifth Discipline* by Peter Senge. This is the book, based on the author's research at MIT Sloan School of Business, that first truly explored the concept of the learning organization, why such an approach is necessary, and how it can be achieved.

Any resource that assists development in the sales area must link to one of the areas upon which development must be focused. You must compile your own list because it must be individual and relate to the job you do and intend to do in the future. General areas may prompt more detailed analysis and so examples are listed here:

» Prospecting techniques
» Making appointments
» Account management
» Account planning
» Opening a sales interview
» Making your case
» Handling objections
» Closing techniques
» Writing sales letters.

To these kinds of factor you need to add, and think about, the most specific level of your own activity. For example, do you have to demonstrate a product, and if so exactly how?

QUALIFICATIONS

There are routes to a variety of qualifications that may act to assist a sales career. Their advantages are essentially threefold. First, they can include content that directly assists with what you need to know and be able to do in order to do either your current, or some future, job. Secondly, they may not just be useful in enabling you to a job, but instrumental in allowing you to qualify for, and be appointed to, a new job. In the second case the fact of studying for, or having passed, some qualification is as important to the situation as the actual practical value of what is learnt. Indeed, the way in which such things enhance your image is certainly a specific consideration. Thirdly, there is the process of undertaking such things. Study may be in a variety of forms, including part time courses and distance learning. But most represent an opportunity to meet others of like mind. These may include people whose brains you can pick or who represent other networking opportunities that are career-enhancing in some way.

Some routes, like a course in say French, may be wholly relevant if that is something you need. Consider two overall categories first.

» *Technical:* a plethora of technical degrees and qualifications may be relevant for you depending upon the field in which you work. Such may range from engineering to topics of much greater complexity.
» *Business:* these also include a wide range of things, from the now ubiquitous MBA to specialist degrees and diplomas with a more direct link to sales.

The first category is too wide to go into here, but two specific bodies are worth noting in the second, both offer professional qualifications and other services and are referred to below under the next heading.

PROFESSIONAL BODIES

The Chartered Institute of Marketing

CIM is the "parent" of the Institute of Professional Sales, listed below (so by all means read about that first), and is listed first as the primary source of reference. As an overall summary CIM describes itself thus:

"The Chartered Institute of Marketing (CIM) is the professional body for marketing, with over 60,000 members worldwide. Founded in 1911, it has been instrumental in elevating marketing to a recognized, respected and chartered profession. It is the only marketing body able to award individual chartered marketer status to eligible members. Chartered marketer status is a professional standard which reflects an individual's commitment to developing their professional skills in an increasingly competitive marketplace. As an examining body for over 60 years, the Institute's certificates and postgraduate diploma (DipM) are internationally recognized qualifications, available through a worldwide network of educational institutions and distance learning providers."

In context here it is worth mentioning certain of their services.

» Career development services which include: a range of information in booklet form or downloadable from their Website; a career advice line, a career counseling service (run in collaboration with Connaught Executive via a network of 25 offices around the UK); and two routes for those seeking new jobs. The first is JobFocus accessed through the institute's Website and is available to all, the second (for members only) is the Job Vacancy Database run with Quantum Consulting Group and accessed via: www.cim.co.uk/membership-net.
» A library and information service.
» Qualifications offered by CIM.
» The network of branches: these mean no one is far from a local source of information and networking (there are a number of overseas branches also and the Institute links with the European Marketing Confederation with associate bodies in 24 countries within and outside the European Union (total membership is more than 300,000). Its Website is www.emc.be.
» CIM Direct: a source of business books for purchase.

Note: while CIM is a source of value to all, you should note that some of the services listed above are available only to members. There are similar bodies in many different countries.

In addition the institute is the parent body for the Institute of Sales Professionals, which undertakes a parallel role but focusing solely on the sales function. It has its own Website: www.iops.co.uk (see below).

The Institute of Professional Sales

This body, effectively a "subsidiary" of the CIM, describes itself as follows.

"The vision of IPS is to create an institute which recognizes both the achievement of professional qualifications and the value of experience. Its aim is to bring together the knowledge of academia, the skills of training organizations, the experience of practitioners with the motivation essential for all selling roles. The objective of IPS is to raise the profile of sales people and to gain recognition for the sales function. In addition, we want to create a very clear training path for those coming in to sales. Additionally, we wanted to provide events and networking opportunities and to define and evolve 'best practice' in sales. Successful selling is essential for any business and the Institute of Professional Sales aims to make selling an accurately defined science rather than just an acquired art.

All the qualifications are based on the national standards together with the real life experience of first class trainers. The corporate benefits offered are that the IPS will recognize training by external companies and help to raise the profile of the sales profession within those companies. IPS is dedicated to raising standards of best practice, is compatible with Investors in People and encompasses many industry leaders. Individual benefits of joining IPS include use of 'designatory letters', advice on career development, Winning Business magazine, an active regional events program and access to an information and library service."

For more information on IPS, visit the Website at www.iops.co.uk or e-mail the Institute at johnmayfield@iops.co.uk. It can be contacted at the same address as The Chartered Institute of Marketing (see above).

Finally, a word about the CAM Foundation (communication, advertising and marketing). CAM is the umbrella body for qualifications across the various marketing disciplines. Its Website can be visited at www.camfoundation.com.

It is also worth mentioning again here that most professional bodies, certainly those offering professional qualifications, have CPD schemes which can be both valuable in their own right and act as a prompt to help create the habit of setting aside regular time for self-development activities.

MAGAZINES

There are many magazines covering the marketing area, either from a general perspective or with a focus on one specific sub-section of marketing, but only a few are of significance and focus on sales.

Winning Business

Quest Media Ltd
9 The Leathermarket
Western Street
London SE1 3ER
Tel: 020 73781188
This is probably the most useful magazine in the field; and not only because I write for it regularly! The publishers describe it thus.

> "Winning Business is a leading edge, bi-monthly magazine pub-
> lished in association with the Institute of Professional Sales,
> targeted at and read by senior managers within organizations that
> have responsibility for customer facing aspects of their business,
> such as sales, marketing and customer service. The uniqueness
> of the publication relates to the fact that it is the only "how to"
> focused magazine in the UK that provides senior management
> with advice, guidance and inspiration to help them win more busi-
> ness. The editorial of the magazine is designed to be of interest to
> any business leader interested in finding, winning, retaining and
> growing business."

The benefits of publishing a magazine that has many of Europe's top business experts writing for it, has enabled the editorial team to build a framework of key business principles around which content is developed. This approach means looking at the subject of how organizations find, win, retain and grow business from three very specific areas, people, processes and technology.

The magazine aims to explore how organizations develop and evolve their people and their processes to increasingly meet and exceed the needs and expectations of customers whilst using technology to enable the changes and developments they wish to make. The other key principle is to encourage organizations to increasingly integrate the different functions of the organizations, particularly their sales, service and marketing operations in order to improve the consistency and the quality of the experience for the customer.

This consistent framework enables the magazine to build on and broaden the range of issues and subjects it addresses whilst continuously questioning the validity of any new ideas and concepts against its core principles.

To achieve its objectives *Winning Business* brings together global experts on sales, service and marketing. They write to a tight brief, resulting in easily accessible, knowledgeable and authoritative editorial that consistently shows its readers how to succeed in their efforts to find, win, retain and grow business with their profitable customers.

The magazine is packed full of advice, ideas, best practice and research identifying and exploring the best and most effective ways for organizations to constantly improve their performance. By providing a reader-friendly package of high quality, interesting, practical, and thought-provoking advice in an expertly written, well-designed format, the magazine captures the attention of senior business leaders, influencing the opinion formers.

Anyone in sales, and aspiring to go higher, would find this interesting.

Sales Director

This is also useful and has very much the style and format of something like the journal *Management Today*.
www.saleszone.co.uk

Sales & Marketing Management

The main US magazine on the subject, its coverage is broader than solely sales management, and containing useful material.
www.salesandmarketing.com

Sales & Marketing Professional

This is the journal linked to the Institute of Sales & Marketing Management. Somehow this has always remained in the shadow of the main institutes. Its base is sales, but it seems to think marketing is sexier and positions itself "higher".

All the above are specific, but it is worth bearing in mind that, as selling is an essential part of the marketing mix, marketing journals feature articles on selling and sales management from time to time. The library at the Chartered Institute of Marketing will produce lists of recent articles on request, though there is a charge to non-members.

Finally, for a general overview of marketing issues (which inevitably touches on sales and business development as a topic), the CIM journal is worth noting.

Marketing Business
Exmouth House
3–11 Pine Street
London EC1R 0JH
Tel: 020 79235400

One source leads to another, and what is most relevant will vary at different times and at different stages of your career. Keep an eye open and pick up on anything that might help you.

RESEARCH

The Future of Selling is a report published late in 2000 by Quest Media Ltd (the publishers of the journal *Winning Business*) in association with the Institute of Professional Selling and consultants Miller Heinman Inc. This is an interesting research study, more so because the area is rarely researched. It reviews current practice and looks to the future examining the changing sales role, customer expectations and beliefs, and the whole way sales teams are organized, staffed, rewarded and managed.

Key findings indicated that:

» Customers are becoming better informed and more organized, demanding and sharp in their dealings with sales people (with the Internet being used to a significant extent for pre-buying research).
» Technology is having, and will continue to have, an effect on sales activity: most dramatically it is replacing sales people with electronic, impersonal, buying, though this is not affecting large numbers of business areas. The dynamic nature of this area is evidenced by the uncertainty the research respondents reflected in their forecasts of what other influences are becoming important.

» Recruitment is a perpetual challenge as is retention.
» CRM is becoming a more widespread basis for many customer interactions, and creating a more formal basis for them.
» Training remains a constant need (and more of it is being done, and the range of ways in which it is done are also increasing) as the level of competency of sales people is seen as key to success.
» Reporting takes a high proportion of working time – reducing sales people's time spent face to face with customers; this despite the increasing computerization of data collection and reporting systems.

Sales management, its practice, manner and style, is seen as significant to success. On the one hand the increasing professionalism of the sales role, and the broadening of sales people's responsibilities in response to market changes, heighten the role and managerial skills sales managers must have. On the other hand, there is one area where sales managers seem to sometimes to be marginalized. This is respect of new technology. For example, sales managers are often not involved in the development of e-business strategies. There are dangers here. An e-business strategy that is not made compatible with traditional sales processes may lack realism. While technology and its development are always difficult to predict, it is perhaps best done in this area with the sales manager's active involvement, or the baby might just get thrown out with the bath water.

The section of the report on the impact of e-commerce is interesting. Just to quote one statistic, 90 per cent of respondents' organizations have a Website; but 57 per cent of them said they were not used to assist sales.

It is a valuable study that deserves to be repeated on a regular basis.

BOOKS

No attempt is made here to recommend a definitive list of books on selling. They are many and varied. They range from the ubiquitous *The One-Minute Sales Person,* and other short books, which either feature one aspect of selling or attempt to encapsulate the process, to heavyweight tomes that review the whole process. If you want a short sharp encapsulation try my own *The Sales Excellence Pocketbook* in the unique Management Pocketbooks format.

What is worth saying is that reading widely is worthwhile. You will not find everything equally useful, but as you come at things in a variety of different way you will encounter useful information and have an increasing basis for applying best practice.

MASTER'S DEGREE

Finally, there is now for the first time in the UK a master's degree in sales management. Designed primarily as a follow on from the Diploma in Professional Sales, it is offered by the University of Portsmouth Business School. The course consists of four modules taken over a fourteen-month period on a part-time basis, designed to allow a job to be largely unaffected. It includes project work and ends with the preparation of a 15–20,000-word dissertation. A good sign, it seems to me, of the increasing acceptance of the importance of sales as a key part of marketing.

Ten Steps to Making Self Development in Sales Work

- » Resolve to be a regular self-developer.
- » Analyze and set clear objectives.
- » Make and use a plan.
- » Create sufficient time.
- » Learn from experience.
- » Learn from others.
- » Spot opportunities.
- » Utilize a mix of methods.
- » Monitor progress.
- » Aim high and be positive.

"The illiterate of the twenty first century will not be those that cannot read and write, but those who cannot learn, unlearn and relearn."

Alvin Toffler

Development ultimately stands or falls on what *you* do. Therefore the attitude you take to it, and the action you take, dictate whether or not it will help you perform as you wish and achieve what you want now and in the future. The following, while not attempting to repeat what has been said elsewhere or be comprehensive, encapsulates under 10 headings the key things that can help you make a success of what you do in development.

1. RESOLVE TO BE A REGULAR SELF DEVELOPER

This may seem an obvious starting point, indeed it is. Most people would agree that development is a "good thing". In surveys about job satisfaction people regularly rate the fact that they want to be learning and moving forward in terms of their capabilities as a prime requirement of a satisfying job (and the same sentiment is also applied to managers – "I want to work for someone who I learn from").

So far so good: development is desirable and to be taken advantage of wherever possible. But this is not sufficient.

As has been made clear throughout the previous text, just taking up opportunities for development is not enough. Taking them up unthinkingly or without considering the development possibilities inherent in them is worse. For example, how many appraisals take place in organizations every day that are no more than going through the motions? They are neither constructive nor likely to lead positively to improved performance in the future. How many of these would be more useful if more thinking and preparation was done?

This is just one example, but it makes a point – you need to take an initiative with development, both with activities on offer, in order to get the best from them, and certainly with the self-development activity that you plan and implement personally. Doing so must become a lifelong habit.

2. ANALYZE AND SET CLEAR OBJECTIVES

This needs a mention and is rightly high on this list of 10 key areas promoting success. The details (set out in Chapter 6) will not be repeated here. Suffice to say that given pressure of time, and perhaps money too, you must have a clear focus for all your development activity.

Without this time can be wasted doing things that, while generally sensible, do not address your specific development objectives sufficiently accurately to be as useful as alternative action. One of the first business maxims ever to become a well-known phrase was: "If you don't know where you are going, any road will do" (Peter Drucker). It makes as much sense for an individual as for a business.

3. MAKE AND USE A PLAN

Plan the work and work the plan, so says the old adage. It is true, it is common sense; yet it is easy to overlook and to regard planning as a chore. A program of self development first needs some analysis and clear objectives (see Chapter 6). A plan – which means something in writing – is actually a time-saving device. It ensures that things are not overlooked, that each activity can be made to relate sensibly to all others, and allows necessary fine-tuning along the way.

A plan should not be a straitjacket. It is more akin to a route map. That allows you to plan an unfamiliar journey, yet also helps if things do not go to plan, for instance allowing revisions to avoid road works or accident. The description, "rolling plan" makes sense here. That is something that is clear in the short term, perhaps specifying one hundred per cent what you intend to do, and which sets out a clear idea of the time beyond – to be filled in progressively as time goes by in the light of actual circumstances.

The rule here is simple: make a plan and put it in writing. The extent of it is actually less important. I know people who plan their development scrupulously in this way and what results is a folder with just a few, perhaps half a dozen, sheets of paper (or a file in a computer that they view on screen). It need not be onerous to create, or voluminous in extent; it is a foundation to what you subsequently do and very valuable in making things happen.

4. CREATE SUFFICIENT TIME

In the modern workplace there never seems to be time for anything. Pressure, stress, meetings, administration, travel and traffic and more (not least customers!) all conspire to keep us on the run. Setting priorities is key. If you do not concentrate on the things that matter most, then you will never get the results that you want.

In selling this is most evident in the area of sales productivity and organization. Deciding whom you see, organizing how many people you see and deciding the frequency with which you see regular contacts all directly impact what your work produces. But there are other priorities too and development is certainly one of them. We are all familiar with the maxim to work smarter, not harder. It is a valid comment. You need to see development, and particularly self development, where you have to find the time yourself, as a means to an end. It is an investment. Time spent now helps make what you do in future more effective; it directly links to the results that you want to achieve. It also links to longer term aims, in that you may never gain the advancement you want if you are constantly failing to fit in actions that would constitute firm stepping stones along the way.

In some organizations development is specifically targeted in time terms. In the financial services area, for example, this it typical – in one organization, Professional Intermediary Services, their sales team must spend 50 hours per year simply to keep their "product knowledge" up to date. So, it will help if you:

» set yourself some sort of target;
» address separately the things you do entirely at your own behest, and those that management initiates and thus allows time for (even if you have help ensure that the initiative takes place); and
» develop and stick with appropriate habits so that some of your self-development becomes a useful routine (for example, dwelling on the lessons from an individual sales meeting for a moment after being with a customer).

Time management is made effective largely through many details. There sadly being no magic formula that produces excellent productivity, making sure that you do not shortchange your development intentions is key to your success.

5. LEARN FROM EXPERIENCE

As the old proverb says: experience is the best teacher. Certainly it is true to say that at the core of self development, separate from any methods, systems and processes is one key thing – you. The attitude you take, and the way in which you harness your experience so that it provides a basis for change and better operation in future, is vital. You can make a real difference.

Looking at the sales process you need a sound understanding of the way it works and what makes it successful, then you have a reference against which to view your own practice and experience. Doing so must become a habit. You need to:

» be conscious of what you do, literally customer by customer, day by day;
» consider – analyze if you like – how particular things go, for instance looking at how you handled a customer visit, how they reacted to what you did and what came of it;
» note areas of note. These may be things that went well that you want to repeat and build on or things that could be better and need consideration, experiment or change; and
» act on this process, adjusting your future approaches taking it into account.

Realistically you are not going to indulge in lengthy contemplation after ever call, but if you can get into the habit of pausing regularly to consider then this is literally invaluable. A similar approach can be brought to bear on every aspect of your job asking yourself questions like: was that course attendance (or appraisal or sales meeting) useful, how did I play it and are there ways in which I can make the next such experience more useful?

Make experience work for you, effectively accelerate it and you have regular, pertinent learning on tap on an ongoing basis. This strengthens the effect of every other aspect of development to which you are exposed.

6. LEARN FROM OTHERS

Your development is sufficiently important to leave no stone unturned in looking for ways of giving it strength. There is no monopoly on knowledge or ability, so you need to be in touch with others who can act as a catalyst to your development process. They can help ensure that you maximize what you achieve and make it easier to do – and perhaps more fun – at the same time. Like so much else this needs some systematic action; it is not simply a matter of tapping any useful people you happen to know. You need to:

» identify those people inside the organization and out that might be able to help you (these include colleagues, management in functions such as HR, opposite numbers in competitors);

» make and maintain contact, have meetings, exchange e-mails and keep in contact on an ongoing basis;

» recognize that such networking must be two-way to be self-sustaining, in other words other people must find their contact with you as useful as yours with them is – give as well as take; and

» link ideas, suggestions and experience gained this way with other activities to maximize its effectiveness; for example use a contact as a sounding board to help prepare a contribution you have planned for a forthcoming sales meeting.

Interesting and valuable alliances are possible. Sometimes it can start with a particular swap: you want to pick brains on one subject and are able to help someone else with advice in another area. Ultimately this overlaps with the idea of mentoring (which is explored in Chapter 6).

7. SPOT OPPORTUNITIES

There is a difference implied here between recognizing opportunities, by which I mean you should see and take advantage of ongoing processes and events like your regular job appraisal, and spotting opportunities. The distinction makes the point that some opportunities are less obvious. Some things are unpredictable and you need the habit of being alert to any possibility that might assist your development plans.

Linked to the idea of keeping an eye out for opportunities should be that of experiment. As just one example, I have sat on various committees over the years and an immediate reaction is that it is not my favorite thing. However, it is something that is, on occasion, worth trying (and saying that you will attend a few times before committing yourself more permanently) and I can think of more than one spell on committees that started somewhat reluctantly but from which I learnt a great deal and met people who were of further assistance.

This is another principle that needs consciously adhering to in the light of a busy life which leaves no room to observe or explore anything but the most obvious.

8. UTILIZE A MIX OF METHODS

There is more to heart surgery than reading a good book. So too with selling: you need to come at it in a number of different ways. First, recognize that there are two paths to development that you can influence:

» taking advantage of things "in place" – from getting the most help from your manager to making appraisals a constructive process; here *self* development adds to a process that would do something anyway and makes sure you obtain maximum benefit; and
» taking an initiative and doing things yourself. Such things may be as simple as reading a book, or as comprehensive and ongoing as studying for a qualification.

Beyond that, there are a number of reasons to make sure that you undertake a mix of things.

» *Different things work in different ways:* a computer based session of some sort may lead you through the facts about something, whereas attending a course allows discussion, is an opportunity to interact with others, and can allow you to test ideas.

» *Sheer variety:* you are more likely to do more and do it more regularly if what you are doing contains some variety; if it is interesting you will be more likely to stick with it.

» *Reinforcement:* repetition is one of the basic tenets of learning. If you are exposed to ideas, techniques, whatever, in a variety of different ways then the key things are more likely to make sense and to stick. If you contrast very different methods, this reinforcement is clear – a factual description on page or screen perhaps reinforced by the humor of a training film on the same topic.

» *Productivity:* realistically you have to mix methods to make an element of self-development possible; to make it fit in with a no-doubt busy work schedule. So a tape you can listen to in the car adds something to what you do with effectively no increase in "development time" (and the traffic may not seem so frustrating!).

In one area variety is helped by change, technology seems to offer new learning methods every day (see Chapter 4).

9. MONITOR PROGRESS

In describing the way in which self development can help you the word systematic has been used a number of times. One element of the systematic approach is that of monitoring progress. The premise here is simple. What you do next should be based on progress to date so as to create a logical continuity of development and progress.

You want to know that progress is being made, and how that is best assisted. So, everything you do should be rated in terms of how it helps. If you go on a course consider if it was useful. Consider also why this was. Was it down to the person who conducted it, the nature or extent of participation or the way it related to your job? Whatever it was there may be things to note and that will affect your future actions – for example, avoiding a particular course leader or resolving to attend more courses using a certain style of approach.

You need to monitor your progress too. If say you are trying to improve the quality of your written reports, then there are a variety of things you can do – but does your report writing change for the better as a result? You need to make, and get from others in many instances, judgments about this sort of progress. Self development is not just a good thing in some academic sense, it is a means to an end and you always need to be sure that you are actually making suitable progress towards those ends.

10. AIM HIGH AND BE POSITIVE

There are many maxims about aiming high, and "positive mental attitude" is not just a state of mind, it is an industry, certainly in the United States. All so obvious, but the dangers are equally real. It is very easy to form clear intentions, take some action but allow an initial lack of success and the ongoing pressure of work to let you sideline them and do little or nothing more. Sustaining a program of self development needs some commitment and some persistence.

If you aim high you may still not achieve the peak of success, but you are more likely to achieve more than you would with lower intentions. There are four manifestations of this.

» *Excellence:* in terms of everything you do and the professionalism with which you do it you should aim for excellence. Getting by is not enough, unless you are ahead of the game, unless you are constantly moving forward you are vulnerable to changing circumstances and what you do may no longer impress customers as it should. In a dynamic environment the status quo is an enemy, as Henry Kaiser said: "You can't sit on the lid of progress. If you do, you will be blown to pieces."

» *Challenge:* you should not rule things out too readily as being beyond you. Only by accepting a challenge will you make progress, and in any case more job satisfaction comes from taking on and making a success of something genuinely challenging than from just "ticking over" and allowing a job to become repetitive.

» *Advancement:* is success in your current job, but success in terms of your longer-term career is another. If you fail to take the necessary early steps then you may effectively block your progress and regret it later. It may seem like a heck of a jump to sales director or managing director, but each step on the way may well prove – or be able to be made – manageable.

» *Skills and techniques:* to do a particular job you need to be able to do, and do well, the things that it necessitates. So you need to take on the challenge of developing new skills. Such things often seem daunting. There was a stage in my career when the last thing I ever thought that I would do, or wanted to do or indeed thought I would be able to do was public speaking. I hated the very idea. But circumstances led me towards it. I had to learn how to do it – and have in fact spent a major part of my subsequent career in training involving speaking to groups of all sizes; and indeed teaching others so to do. Again you must not rule out areas of development for the wrong reasons; and these include distaste for them or a lack of confidence in your ability to do them. Aiming high includes embracing the acquisition of all the skills that will take you where you want to go.

Certainly all this demands a positive attitude. "If you think you can, you can and if you think you can't, you're right (Mary Kay Ash). Fair comment. So, be positive about your selling and your ability to satisfy customers. Be positive about your ability to succeed and make progress. Of course, as this text has made clear, you need to work at it and do so in a considered and systematic way. Success does not just happen, but you can make it happen and your attitude to and action regarding self development is a key part of what allows you to do so.

It is an old saying, originally attributed to Vidal Sassoon, and still worth noting: "The only place where success comes before work is in the dictionary."

True enough, the trick is to recognize the fact and work at it, but also to make the work necessary as painless as possible. Well-chosen self-development activity needs exactly this approach. Thereafter it is how you proceed next that matters. Remember what Kahil Gibran said: "A little knowledge that *acts* is worth infinitely more than much knowledge that is idle." The final quotes are chosen to help aim you in precisely this direction.

"If a little knowledge is dangerous, where is the man who has so much as to be out of danger?"

T.H. Huxley

"Companies can't promise lifetime employment, but by constant training and education we may be able to guarantee lifetime employability."

Jack Welch, CEO General Electric Company

"Ideas are somewhat like babies – they are born small, immature and shapeless. They are promise rather than fulfillment. In the innovative company executives do not say, 'This is a damn-fool idea'. Instead they ask 'What would be needed to make this embryonic, half-baked, foolish idea into something that makes sense, that is an opportunity for us?'"

Peter Drucker, management guru and author

"Imagination is the beginning of creation. You imagine what you desire, you will what you imagine and at last you create what you will."

George Bernard Shaw

"If one wants to be successful, one must think. One must think until it hurts. One must worry a problem in one's mind until it seems there cannot be another aspect of it that hasn't been considered."

Lord Thomson of Fleet

"Hitch your wagon to a star; keep your nose to the grindstone; put your shoulder to the wheel; keep an ear to the ground and watch for writing on the wall."

Herbert Prochnow, former president, First National Bank of Chicago

Frequently Asked Questions (FAQs)

Q1: What exactly is self development?

A: See Chapter 1 which defines the process and puts it in context of the wider issues of training and development.

Q2: Is self development in sales necessary?

A: For real success it certainly is, and a reading of Chapters 1 and 2 will show just why.

Q3: How do I decide what to do?

A: See Chapters 6 and 7 linking action and career development intentions.

Q4: From how far afield can I learn?

A: See Chapter 5 on the global implications of self development.

Q5: Is the need for self development becoming more or less important?

A: See Chapter 3 which examines the evolution of the process.

Q6: Is this something that the IT revolution helps?

A: See Chapter 4, The E-dimension.

Q7: What do other people do?

A: See Chapter 7, Self Development In Practice.

Q8: How can I be sure I am doing the things that will help me most?

A: See Chapter 7, Self Development In Practice.

Q9: Where can I find out more?

A: See Chapter 9, Self Development Resources.

Q10: I'm busy just doing the job, where can I get to the key issues – fast?

A: See Chapter 10–10 Steps to Making Self Development Work.

Acknowledgments

I can claim no credit for the origination of the unique format of the series of which this work is part. So thanks are due to those at Capstone who did so, and for the opportunity they provided for me to play a small part in so significant and novel a publishing project.

No book is entirely a solo enterprise and this one is no exception. My early career involved me in selling and my move into consultancy and training both kept me selling and involved me in the process in a rather different way. Any writing I have done about selling, including this volume and another ExpressExec title *Selling Services*, has been made possible because of my contact with a host of people: colleagues, clients, attendees on training courses I have conducted and even those sales people I have myself bought from or refused to buy from. I have learnt from them throughout my career, and continue to do so. Though too numerous to list, I am indebted to them all.

Patrick Forsyth
Touchstone Training & Consultancy
28 Saltcote Maltings
Maldon
Essex CM9 4QP
United Kingdom.

Index

EXPRESSEXEC –
BUSINESS THINKING AT YOUR FINGERTIPS

ExpressExec is a 12-module resource with 10 titles in each module. Combined they form a complete resource of current business practice. Each title enables the reader to quickly understand the key concepts and models driving management thinking today.

Available from:
www.expressexec.com

Customer Service Department
John Wiley & Sons Ltd
Southern Cross Trading Estate
1 Oldlands Way, Bognor Regis
West Sussex, PO22 9SA
Tel: +44(0)1243 843 294
Fax: +44(0)1243 843 303
Email: cs-books@wiley.co.uk

Printed and bound by CPI Group (UK) Ltd, Croydon, CR0 4YY

Printed and bound by CPI Group (UK) Ltd, Croydon, CR0 4YY

13/04/2025

14656462-0002